My KOREAN TUTOR for Ultimate Beginners

DARAKWON

Preface

안녕하세요!

Welcome to your first step into learning Korean!

One of the most important aspects of language learning is maintaining confidence and motivation. This book is therefore designed not to dwell too much on "perfect" grammar, but rather to help you enjoy the process by imagining yourself using Korean in real-life situations. With this book, you will quickly learn Hangeul, the Korean writing system, and then progress to essential expressions that you can apply in everyday life. This book is made up of three parts.

In **PART 1 : 한글 Hangeul**, you'll learn the Korean alphabet step by step. You'll start with the basics of Hangeul and move on to reading and writing consonants and vowels, as well as practicing common words and greetings. Follow along with the handwriting guide videos to make writing Hangeul easier. Every character, word, and greeting comes with audio, so you can listen and repeat as much as you like.

In **PART 2 : Essential Patterns**, you'll learn the basic grammar elements that make up Korean sentences, along with key expression patterns that are used in everyday life. Instead of focusing on difficult grammar terms or detailed analysis, we explain everything through clear and simple patterns that are easy to understand. You'll practice these patterns with a variety of exercises designed to help you absorb them quickly. Use the clear English explanations to build a strong foundation, and try applying what you've learned right away through practice questions. To support your understanding, we also provide short video lectures by the author. Even if you're new to grammar, you'll be able to build accurate Korean sentences with confidence.

In **PART 3 : Let's Talk! Real Situations**, you'll get to put everything you've learned into practice through real-life conversations. You'll pick up natural expressions that Korean speakers actually use in daily life, and practice through 27 practical dialogues based on common situations. Listen to the audio files and repeat as much as you like. You can also try writing out the conversations and rearranging the sentences to build fluency in the "Structure Review" section. Through these steps, you'll strengthen your foundation and feel ready to speak Korean more naturally and confidently.

By the time you reach the end of the book, you'll be surprised at how much Korean you've learned! We hope this book becomes a reliable and encouraging guide on your Korean learning journey. Let's get started together!

Saemi Park, Kyuin Kim

How to Use This Book

PART 1 : 한글 Hangeul

Part 1 is where you will learn the Korean alphabet, Hangeul. Starting with the basic consonants and vowels, you will move on to compound letters, final consonants, and double final consonants. Step by step, you will build a strong foundation in Hangeul.

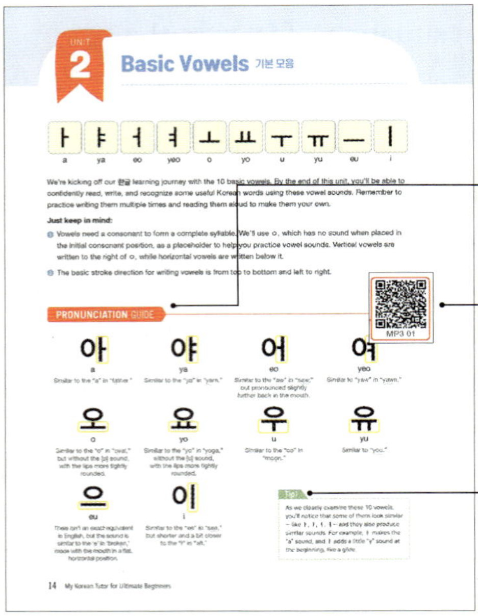

PRONUNCIATION GUIDE

Korean sounds are explained in an easy way by connecting them to similar English sounds.

MP3 QR

Scan the MP3 QR codes to listen and repeat for practice.

Tip!

Here you can find extra explanations about sounds that learners often find confusing or hard to pronounce. These tips will help you pronounce Korean more accurately.

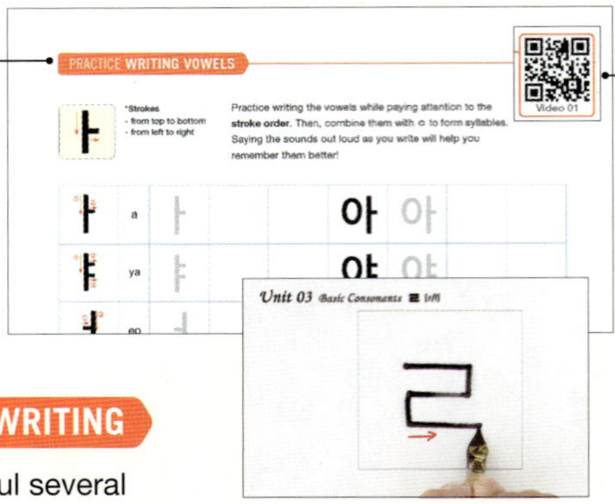

PRACTICE WRITING

Write Hangeul several times in the correct stroke order to get used to it.

VIDEO QR

Scan the video QR codes to access helpful videos.

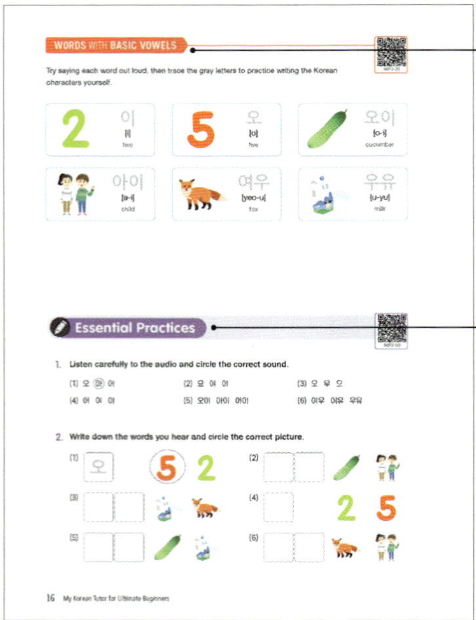

WORDS

Read and write words using the letters you learned.

Essential Practices

Test yourself with review questions to see how much you remember. Answers are in the appendix.

PART 2 : Essential Patterns

In Part 2, you will learn the basic expressions and grammar patterns that are most often used in real conversations. Explanations are simple and easy to follow, so you can quickly use what you learn in sentences and short dialogues.

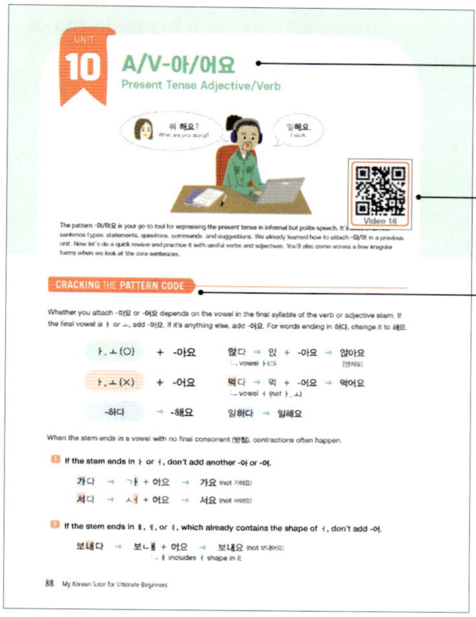

INTRODUCTION

Take a moment to look at the Unit title and picture first. By looking at the picture and speech bubbles, you can get a sense of how each expression is used in real-life conversations.

SHORT LECTURE VIDEO

Scan the QR code to watch a short video lectures for this Unit.

CRACKING THE PATTERN CODE

Here you will see how each grammar pattern is built, with simple diagrams and clear explanations. We use easy and visual explanations so you can quickly understand the structure.

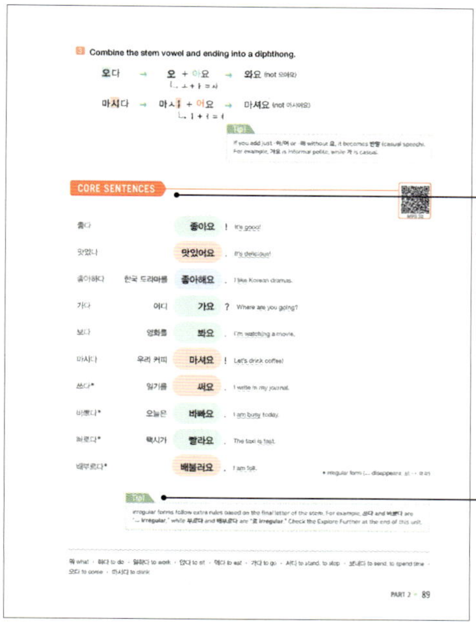

CORE SENTENCES

These sentences show the key patterns in action. Pay attention to how each form is constructed, and practice by listening and repeating several times.

Tip!

Here you will find helpful explanations to support your understanding, along with related expressions.

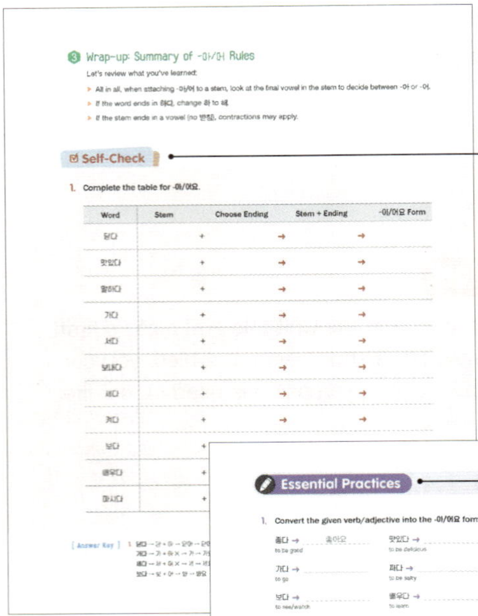

Self-Check

Use quick review questions to check what you've learned so far. Compare your answers with the key below to make sure you understand before moving on.

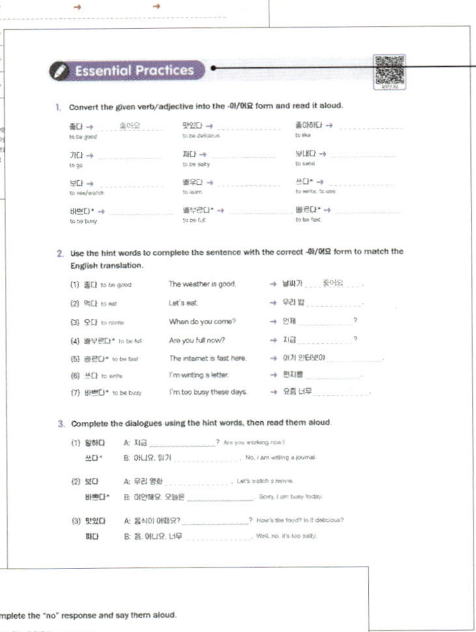

Essential Practices

Practice using what you've learned, changing it into your "own words" through different exercises. Practice usually has three steps—Warm-up → Sentence Building → Creating a Conversation—so you can move smoothly from simple changes to short dialogues.

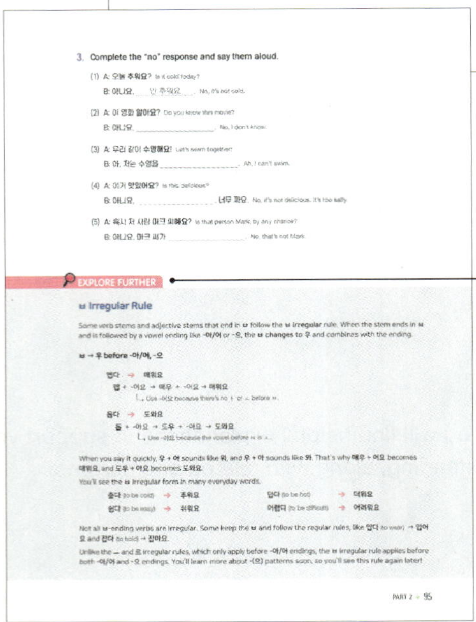

Explore Further

Take one more step by exploring additional grammar notes, cultural background, and related expressions. This will help you understand Korean more deeply and connect it naturally to its real-life usage.

PART 3 : Let's Talk! Real Situations

In Part 3, you will put everything you've learned into practice with real speaking exercises. Practice dialogues based on everyday situations, and use the expressions you've studied in real-life contexts to gain confidence in speaking Korean.

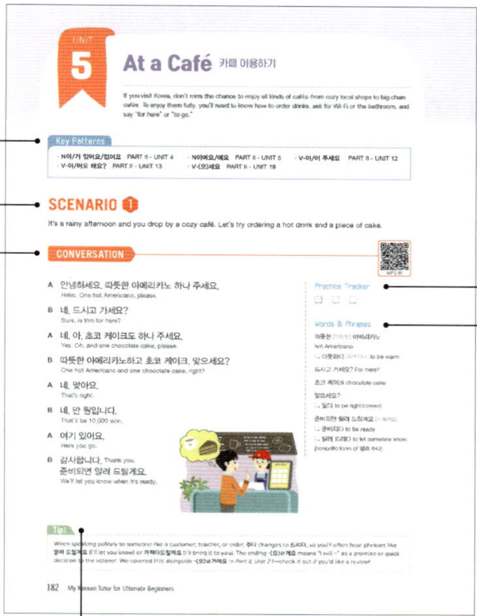
UNIT 5 At a Café 카페 이용하기

Key Patterns

SCENARIO 1

CONVERSATION

A 안녕하세요. 따뜻한 아메리카노 하나 주세요.

B 네. 드시고 가세요?

A 네. 아, 초코 케이크도 하나 주세요.

B 따뜻한 아메리카노하고 초코 케이크, 맞으세요?

A 네. 맞아요.

B 네. 만 원입니다.

A 여기 있어요.

B 감사합니다. 준비되면 알려 드릴게요.

Practice Tracker

Words & Phrases

Tip!

Key Patterns

Each Unit begins with the key patterns used in the dialogues. If you'd like, you can go back to Part 2 to review the patterns before practicing the conversations.

SCENARIO

Each Unit has three different scenarios. Before reading the dialogue, look at the short situation description and imagine what you might say in that situation.

CONVERSATION

Read the dialogue for the scenario out loud first, then scan the MP3 QR code to listen to the audio and practice speaking along. Check how the grammar is used in the dialogues.

Practice Tracker

Keep track of how many times you've practiced listening and speaking.

Words & Phrases

Check the meaning of the key words and expressions from the dialogue, and review them whenever you need.

Tip!

Here you can find extra notes about useful variations, detailed explanations, or cultural context for expressions in the dialogues. This will help you expand your knowledge and speak more naturally.

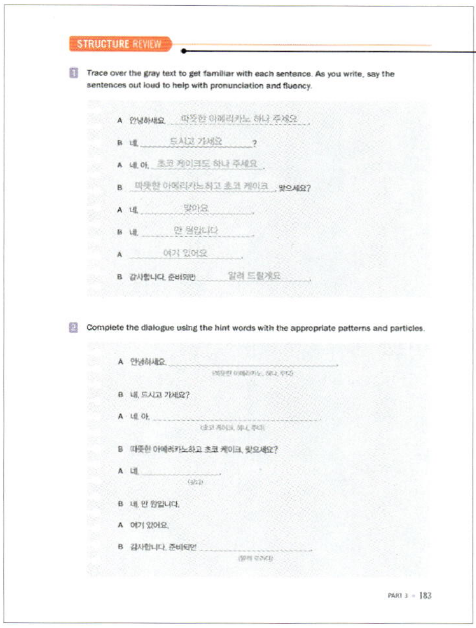
STRUCTURE REVIEW

1 Trace over the gray text to get familiar with each sentence. As you write, say the sentences out loud to help with pronunciation and fluency.

2 Complete the dialogue using the hint words with the appropriate patterns and particles.

STRUCTURE REVIEW

Rewrite and transform the important sentences from the dialogues. By first organizing the flow and structure in writing, you'll feel more prepared for speaking practice.

APPENDIX

- Answers
- Index

Contents

PART 3

APPENDIX

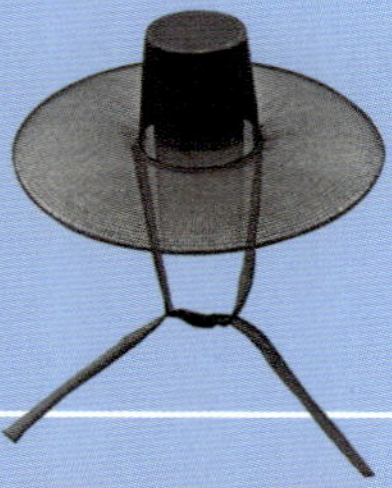

PART 1

한글 Hangeul

Have you ever found yourself staring at Korean words on a menu, in a drama, or on a K-pop video—wondering what they mean or how they sound? Maybe you've wanted to read a sign in Korean without needing Roman letters, or say a Korean word with confidence instead of guessing how it's pronounced.

By the end of this part, you'll be able to read Korean words confidently. 한글 (Hangeul) is actually simple and logical. With a little practice, you'll be surprised at how quickly you can start reading on your own.

This part includes a variety of words to help you practice different sounds. Key vocabulary comes with pictures and meanings, while other words are for pronunciation practice. There's no need to memorize every word. Just enjoy saying the sounds and focus on the ones with pictures and meanings.

UNIT 1

Basic Knowledge on Hangeul 한글 기본 지식

The Invented Writing System, 한글 (Hangeul)

한글 is the name of the Korean alphabet. Unlike many other writing systems, 한글 was not adapted from another script or influenced by long-standing tradition. Instead, it was scientifically designed in 1443 under the guidance of King Sejong the Great and his scholars. It was officially distributed to the public in 1446. King Sejong's vision was to make reading and writing accessible to everyone, regardless of their social status or educational background. This makes 한글 easy to learn for beginners yet versatile enough to express complex ideas.

Did you know that Korea even has a national holiday to celebrate 한글's invention? **Hangeul Day** is celebrated on October 9th every year with various events commemorating its creation and contributions to Korean culture. This goes to show how remarkable 한글 is — the writing system's creator is known and the system is cherished enough to have its own holiday.

One Letter, One Sound

The greatest advantage of 한글 might be this: its one-to-one correspondence between letters and sounds. Each character directly represents a sound, which makes reading and pronunciation easier for beginners.

In English, the same letter can represent different sounds depending on the word. For example, in "circle," the first "c" sounds like "s," while the second sounds like "k." The vowel "a" is also pronounced differently in "cat" and "ace." This variety is a natural feature of English spelling and pronunciation.

한글, however, was designed to be simple and consistent: each letters largely correspond to single sound. That way, you can spend less time memorizing and more time learning how consonants and vowels work together to form syllables.

Vowels and Consonants: C+V(+C) Syllables

한글 consists of **21 vowels and 19 consonants**, making a total of 40 letters. At first glance, this might seem overwhelming, but don't worry! We'll start by learning the 10 basic vowels and 10 basic consonants, with clearly distinct shapes. From there, you'll gradually learn how these basic letters evolve into more complex ones. If you follow along step by step, you'll find it easy to master 한글.

한글 syllables are written in blocks, with each block representing one syllable. Each syllable always consists of **at least one consonant (C) and one vowel (V)**. Sometimes, an additional consonant, called a final consonant, 받침 (batchim), is added at the bottom.

The arrangement of these blocks depends on the shape of the vowel.

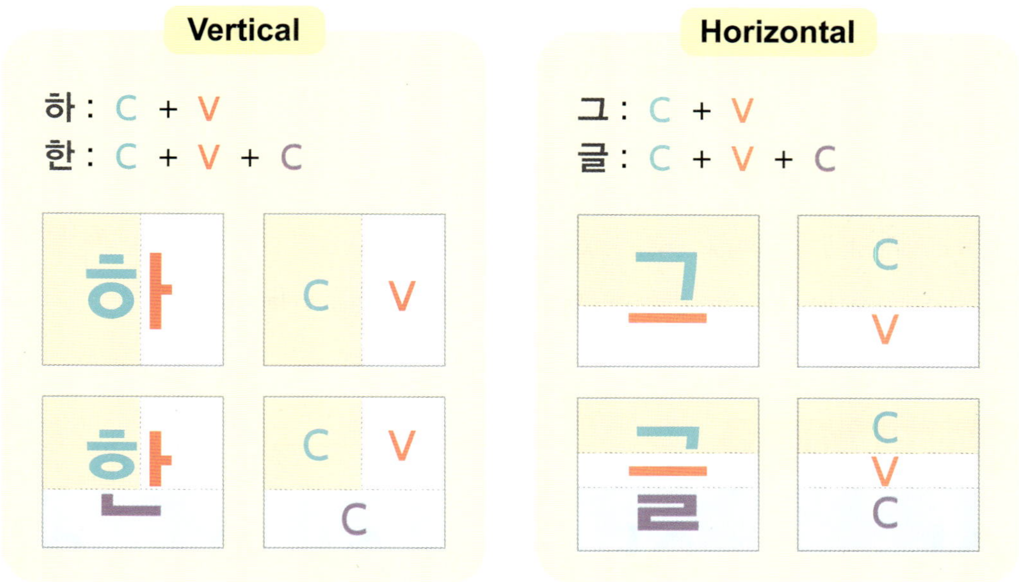

- **Vertical Vowels** When the vowel is vertical (e.g., ㅏ, ㅓ, ㅣ), the consonant is placed to the left of the vowel.
  - ▸ 하 (C + V)
  - ▸ 한 (C + V + final consonant ㄴ)
- **Horizontal Vowels** When the vowel is horizontal (e.g., ㅗ, ㅜ, ㅡ), the consonant is placed above the vowel.
  - ▸ 그 (C + V)
  - ▸ 글 (C + V + final consonant ㄹ)

This logical structure ensures that syllables remain compact, balanced, and easy to read, regardless of their complexity.

UNIT 2

Basic Vowels 기본 모음

ㅏ	ㅑ	ㅓ	ㅕ	ㅗ	ㅛ	ㅜ	ㅠ	ㅡ	ㅣ
a	ya	eo	yeo	o	yo	u	yu	eu	i

We're kicking off our 한글 learning journey with the 10 basic vowels. By the end of this unit, you'll be able to confidently read, write, and recognize some useful Korean words using these vowel sounds. Remember to practice writing them multiple times and reading them aloud to make them your own.

Just keep in mind:

1. Vowels need a consonant to form a complete syllable. We'll use ㅇ, which has no sound when placed in the initial consonant position, as a placeholder to help you practice vowel sounds. Vertical vowels are written to the right of ㅇ, while horizontal vowels are written below it.
2. The basic stroke direction for writing vowels is from top to bottom and left to right.

PRONUNCIATION GUIDE

MP3 01

아
a
Similar to the "a" in "father."

야
ya
Similar to the "ya" in "yarn."

어
eo
Similar to the "aw" in "saw," but pronounced slightly further back in the mouth.

여
yeo
Similar to "yaw" in "yawn."

오
o
Similar to the "o" in "oval," but without the [ʊ] sound, with the lips more tightly rounded.

요
yo
Similar to the "yo" in "yoga," without the [ʊ] sound, with the lips more tightly rounded.

우
u
Similar to the "oo" in "moon."

유
yu
Similar to "you."

으
eu
There isn't an exact equivalent in English, but the sound is similar to the 'e' in 'broken,' made with the mouth in a flat, horizontal position.

이
i
Similar to the "ee" in "see," but shorter and a bit closer to the "i" in "sit."

Tip!

As we closely examine these 10 vowels, you'll notice that some of them look similar — like ㅏ, ㅑ, ㅓ, ㅕ — and they also produce similar sounds. For example, ㅏ makes the "a" sound, and ㅑ adds a little "y" sound at the beginning, like a glide.

PRACTICE WRITING VOWELS

Video 01

ㅏ

*Strokes
- from top to bottom
- from left to right

Practice writing the vowels while paying attention to the **stroke order**. Then, combine them with ㅇ to form syllables. Saying the sounds out loud as you write will help you remember them better!

ㅏ	a	ㅏ			아	아		
ㅑ	ya	ㅑ			야	야		
ㅓ	eo	ㅓ			어	어		
ㅕ	yeo	ㅕ			여	여		
ㅗ	o	ㅗ			오	오		
ㅛ	yo	ㅛ			요	요		
ㅜ	u	ㅜ			우	우		
ㅠ	yu	ㅠ			유	유		
ㅡ	eu	ㅡ			으	으		
ㅣ	i	ㅣ			이	이		

WORDS WITH BASIC VOWELS

Try saying each word out loud, then trace the gray letters to practice writing the Korean characters yourself.

MP3 02

2	이 [i] two	
5	오 [o] five	
	오이 [o-i] cucumber	
	아이 [a-i] child	
	여우 [yeo-u] fox	
	우유 [u-yu] milk	

Essential Practices

MP3 03

1. Listen carefully to the audio and circle the correct sound.

(1) 오 (아) 어 (2) 요 야 이 (3) 오 우 으

(4) 어 여 야 (5) 오이 아이 어이 (6) 여우 이유 우유

2. Write down the words you hear and circle the correct picture.

(1) [오] (5) 2

(2) [ ][ ]  

(3) [ ][ ]  

(4) [ ] 2 5

(5) [ ][ ]  

(6) [ ][ ]  

UNIT 3

Basic Consonants

기본 자음

ㄱ	ㄴ	ㄷ	ㄹ	ㅁ	ㅂ	ㅅ	ㅇ	ㅈ	ㅎ
g/k	n	d/t	r/l	m	b/p	s	silent/ng	j/ch	h

In Korean, consonants and vowels come together to form syllable blocks. Each block begins with a consonant, followed by a vowel, and sometimes ends with another consonant (C+V+C). For now, let's focus on how consonants sound at the beginning of a syllable.

PRONUNCIATION GUIDE

MP3 04

ㄱ
g/k
가 [ga]
A sound between "g" in "go" and "k" in "kite."

ㄴ
n
나 [na]
Similar to the "n" in "no." It's made by touching your tongue to the upper gums.

ㄷ
d/t
다 [da]
A sound between "d" in "dog" and a soft "t" in "top."

ㄹ
r/l
라 [r/la]
A mix between the "r" in "run" and a light "l" sound in "lip." The tongue lightly taps the roof of the mouth.

ㅁ
m
마 [ma]
Similar to the "m" in "mom." It's made by pressing both lips together.

ㅂ
b/p
바 [ba]
A sound between "b" in "boy" and a soft "p" in "pie."

ㅅ
s
사 [sa]
Similar to the "s" in "sun," but a little softer. Before the vowel ㅣ (i), it can sound slightly like "sh."

ㅇ
silent/ng
아 [a]
Silent at the beginning of a syllable (placeholder). At the end of a syllable, it sounds like "ng" in "song."

ㅈ
j/ch
자 [ja]
A sound between "j" in "jam" and a soft "ch" in "chop." It often sounds closer to "j" between vowels.

ㅎ
h
하 [ha]
Similar to the "h" in "hat," with a light breathy sound.

PRACTICE **WRITING CONSONANTS**

Video 02

Practice writing the basic consonants with the correct stroke order. Then add ㅏ to make syllables like 가, 나, and 다. Say each one out loud as you write.

Some consonants, like ㅅ, ㅈ, and ㅎ, may look a bit different in certain fonts.

ㅅ or ㅅ　　ㅈ or ㅈ　　ㅎ or ㅎ

ㄱ	g/k	ㄱ			가	가		
ㄴ	n	ㄴ			나	나		
ㄷ	d/t	ㄷ			다	다		
ㄹ	r/l	ㄹ			라	라		
ㅁ	m	ㅁ			마	마		
ㅂ	b/p	ㅂ			바	바		
ㅅ	s	ㅅ			사	사		
ㅇ	silent /ng	ㅇ			아	아		
ㅈ	j/ch	ㅈ			자	자		
ㅎ	h	ㅎ			하	하		

WORDS WITH BASIC CONSONANTS

MP3 05

Try saying each word out loud, then trace the gray letters to practice writing the Korean characters yourself.

나

[na]

I, me

너

[neo]

you

비

[bi]

rain

우리

[u-ri]

we, us

머리

[meo-ri]

head, hair

마셔요

[ma-syeo-yo]

I drink.

나무

[na-mu]

tree, wood

구두

[gu-du]

dress shoes

두부

[du-bu]

tofu

아기

[a-gi]

baby

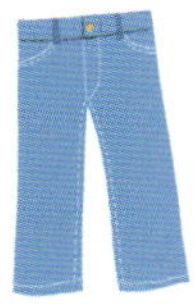

바지

[ba-ji]

pants

휴지

[hyu-ji]

tissue, toilet paper

고구마

[go-gu-ma]

sweet potato

아버지

[a-beo-ji]

father

어머니

[eo-meo-ni]

mother

요리사

[yo-ri-sa]

cook, chef

Essential Practices

MP3 06

1. Listen carefully to the audio and circle the correct sound.

(1) 가 바 라

(2) 지 비 디

(3) 시 히 니

(4) 허 서 저

(5) 나비 루비 보리

(6) 머리 소리 다리

(7) 가다 사다 보다

(8) 소나무 소나기 도자기

2. Write down the words you hear and circle the correct picture.

(1)  

(2)  

(3)  

(4)  

(5)  

(6)  

3. Listen carefully and try writing the words in 한글. Use the picture as a hint!

(1) 

(2) 

(3) 

(4) 

(5) 

(6) 

UNIT 4

Aspirated Consonants & Tense Consonants 거센소리 & 된소리

ㅋ	ㅌ	ㅍ	ㅊ	&	ㄲ	ㄸ	ㅃ	ㅆ	ㅉ
k	t	p	ch		kk	tt	pp	ss	jj

You might notice these look like the basic ones: ㄱ, ㄷ, ㅂ, ㅅ, and ㅈ. Yes, they're related! Aspirated consonants (ㅋ, ㅌ, ㅍ, ㅊ) have an extra stroke and are pronounced with a puff of air. Tense consonants (ㄲ, ㄸ, ㅃ, ㅆ, ㅉ) look like doubles and are also called "double consonants." In this book, we call them "tense consonants" because they're pronounced with more tension, like a tight, squeezed sound.

PRONUNCIATION GUIDE

MP3 07

Aspirated Consonants

Aspirated consonants are sounds made with a strong puff of air. You can feel the air if you hold your hand in front of your mouth when saying them.

ㄱ → ㅋ	ㄷ → ㅌ	ㅂ → ㅍ	ㅈ → ㅊ
g/k → k	d/t → t	b/p → p	j/ch → ch
가 [ga] → 카 [ka]	다 [da] → 타 [ta]	바 [ba] → 파 [pa]	자 [ja] → 차 [cha]
Similar to the "k" in "king," with a strong puff of air.	Similar to the "t" in "tie," with a strong puff of air.	Similar to the "p" in "pie," with a strong puff of air.	Similar to the "ch" in "chat," with a strong puff of air.

Tip!

It may be tricky to distinguish them at the beginning of a word, but remember: basic consonants are far more common.

Tense Consonants

Tense consonants are pronounced with tighter, more constricted sounds. If this is difficult, try adding a very small schwa sound [ə] before the consonant, then pronounce it forcefully. When writing the pronunciation in English, we'll use doubled letters, like ㄲ = "kk" and ㄸ = "tt."

ㄱ → ㄲ	ㄷ → ㄸ	ㅂ → ㅃ	ㅅ → ㅆ	ㅈ → ㅉ
g/k → kk	d/t → tt	b/p → pp	s → ss	j/ch → jj
가 [ga] → 까 [kka]	다 [da] → 따 [tta]	바 [ba] → 빠 [ppa]	사 [sa] → 싸 [ssa]	자 [ja] → 짜 [jja]
Similar to the tense "k" sound in "skill" or "sky," where there's no puff of air.	Similar to the tense "t" sound in "style" or "star," where there's no puff of air.	Similar to the tense "p" sound in "speak" or "spoon," where there's no puff of air.	Similar to the tense "s" sound in "sun," but with more tension.	A tense "j" sound, stronger than "j" in "judge," with no puff of air.

PRACTICE WRITING ASPIRATED CONSONANTS & TENSE CONSONANTS

Video 03

Practice writing the aspirated and tense consonants, and combine them with the basic vowels. Say the sounds out loud as you write to get used to the pronunciation.

Aspirated Consonants

			ㅏ	ㅓ	ㅗ	ㅜ	ㅡ	ㅣ
ㅋ	k	ㅋ	카					
ㅌ	t	ㅌ			토			
ㅍ	p	ㅍ				푸		
ㅊ	ch	ㅊ					츠	

Tense Consonants

			ㅏ	ㅓ	ㅗ	ㅜ	ㅡ	ㅣ
ㄲ	kk	ㄲ	까					
ㄸ	tt	ㄸ		떠				
ㅃ	pp	ㅃ			뽀			
ㅆ	ss	ㅆ				쑤		
ㅉ	jj	ㅉ					쯔	

WORDS WITH ASPIRATED CONSONANTS & TENSE CONSONANTS

MP3 08

Try saying each word out loud, then trace the gray letters to practice writing the Korean characters yourself.

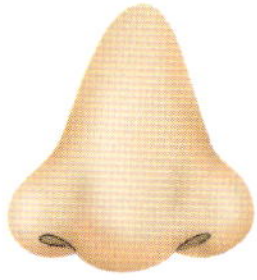

코
[ko]
nose

차
[cha]
tea, car

표
[pyo]
ticket

티셔츠
[ti-syeo-cheu]
T-shirt

카드
[ka-deu]
card

커피
[keo-pi]
coffee

치마
[chi-ma]
skirt

토끼
[to-kki]
rabbit

아빠
[a-ppa]
dad

오빠
[o-ppa]
older brother (for females)

싸다
[ssa-da]
to be cheap

비싸다
[bi-ssa-da]
to be expensive

가짜
[ga-jja]
fake

짜다
[jja-da]
to be salty

코끼리
[ko-kki-ri]
elephant

머리띠
[meo-ri-tti]
hairband

Essential Practices

MP3 09

1. Listen carefully to the audio and circle the correct sound.

(1) 키 끼

(2) 시 씨

(3) 고리 꼬리

(4) 타다 따다

(5) 벼 펴 뼈

(6) 자요 차요 짜요

2. Write down the words you hear and circle the correct picture.

(1) ☐  

(2) ☐  

(3) ☐ 다 

(4) ☐☐  

(5) ☐☐☐ 

(6) ☐☐☐  

3. Listen carefully and try writing the words in 한글. Use the picture as a hint!

(1)  ☐☐

(2)  ☐☐☐

(3)  ☐☐☐

UNIT 5

Complex Vowels

복합 모음

ㅐ	ㅔ	ㅒ	ㅖ	ㅘ	ㅙ	ㅚ	ㅝ	ㅞ	ㅟ	ㅢ
ae	e	yae	ye	wa	wae	oe	weo	we	wi	eui

Complex vowels are made by combining basic vowels to form new sounds. Most are sounds you already know, and some sound almost identical even to native speakers.

MP3 10

PRONUNCIATION GUIDE

Check how each complex vowel combines with a consonant to form different syllables. Just like with basic vowels, we'll use the silent consonant ㅇ as a placeholder to help you practice complex vowel sounds.

애
ae [e]
Similar to "a" in "cat."

에
e [e]
Similar to "e" in "met."

얘
i + ae → yae [ye]
Similar to "yeah."

예
i + e → ye [ye]
Similar to "ye" in "yes."

* Technically, ㅐ and ㅔ were once pronounced differently, but most speakers now pronounce both as [e]. The same goes for ㅒ and ㅖ, which are both pronounced [ye].

와
o + a → wa
Say ㅗ and ㅏ quickly together. It sounds like the beginning of "wow," but without the ending [ʊ].

왜
o + ae → wae [wae]
Say ㅗ and ㅐ quickly together. It's like the beginning of "whale."

외
o + e → oe [wae]
Say ㅗ and ㅔ quickly together. It sounds like "wea" in "weather."

* ㅙ, ㅚ, and ㅞ are all pronounced [wae]. The spelling is different, but the pronunciation is the same. ㅚ is not a combination of ㅗ and ㅣ sounds.

워
u + eo → weo
Say ㅜ and ㅓ quickly together. Similar to "wo" in "wonder."

웨
u + e → we [wae]
Say ㅜ and ㅔ quickly together. Again, like "wea" in "weather."

위
u + i → wi
Say ㅜ and ㅣ quickly together. Similar to "wee" in "week."

의
eu + i → eui
This is a unique sound. Start with ㅡ (mouth flat), then glide to ㅣ.

Tip!

The vowel ㅢ can be pronounced [이] depending on its position in a word. At the beginning of a word, it is always pronounced [의], as in 의자 [의자]. In the middle of a word, it can be [의] or [이], as in 주의 [주의] or [주이]. After a consonant, it is pronounced [이], as in 희망 [히망] or 무늬 [무니].

PRACTICE WRITING COMPLEX VOWELS

Video 04

Practice writing the complex vowels with the correct stroke order. Then add ㅇ to make syllables and say each one out loud as you write.

ㅐ	ae	ㅐ			애	애		
ㅒ	yae [ye]	ㅒ			얘	얘		
ㅔ	e	ㅔ			에	에		
ㅖ	ye	ㅖ			예	예		
ㅘ	wa	ㅘ			와	와		
ㅙ	wae	ㅙ			왜	왜		
ㅚ	oe [wae]	ㅚ			외	외		
ㅝ	weo	ㅝ			워	워		
ㅞ	we [wae]	ㅞ			웨	웨		
ㅟ	wi	ㅟ			위	위		
ㅢ	eui	ㅢ			의	의		

WORDS WITH COMPLEX VOWELS

MP3 11

Try saying each word out loud, then trace the gray letters to practice writing the Korean characters yourself.

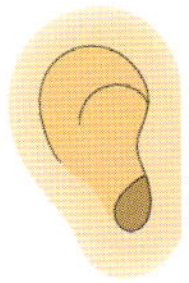

귀
[gwi]
ear

왜
[wae]
why

뭐
[mweo]
what

가게
[ga-ge]
shop, store

시계
[si-gye]
clock, watch

얘기
[yae-gi]
talk, story
(shortened form of 이야기)

사과
[sa-gwa]
apple

돼지
[dwae-ji]
pig

회사
[hoe-sa]
company

의사
[eui-sa]
doctor

의자
[eui-ja]
chair

무지개
[mu-ji-gae]
rainbow

추워요
[chu-weo-yo]
It's cold.

더워요
[deo-weo-yo]
It's hot.

매워요
[mae-weo-yo]
It's spicy.

스웨터
[seu-we-teo]
sweater

Essential Practices

MP3 12

1. Combine consonants and vowels to form syllables.

(1) ㅅ + ㅡ + ㅇ + ㅞ + ㅌ + ㅓ → 스웨터 (sweater)

(2) ㅊ + ㅔ + ㄹ + ㅣ → ______ (cherry)

(3) ㅋ + ㅣ + ㅇ + ㅟ → ______ (kiwi)

(4) ㅅ + ㅑ + ㅇ + ㅝ → ______ (shower)

(5) ㅋ + ㅐ + ㄴ + ㅏ + ㄷ + ㅏ → ______ (Canada)

(6) ㅇ + ㅞ + ㅇ + ㅣ + ㅌ + ㅓ → ______ (waiter)

2. Listen carefully to the audio and circle the correct sound.

(1) 에 예

(2) 얘 왜

(3) 외 와

(4) 에 웨

(5) 와 워

(6) 의 위

3. Write down the words you hear and circle the correct picture.

(1) ☐ 

(2) ☐ 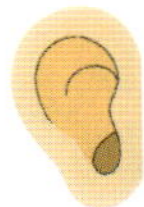 

(3) 시 ☐ 

(4) ☐ 사 

(5) 추 ☐ 요  

(6) ☐ 지  

(7) ☐☐  

(8) ☐☐☐  

UNIT 6

Final Consonants "받침"

받침

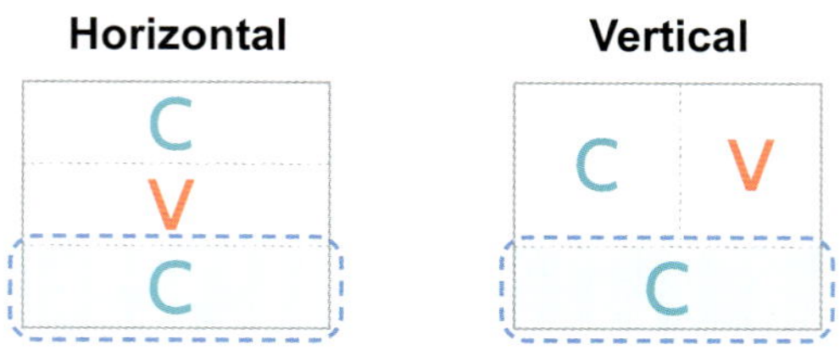

A Korean syllable block can have up to three parts: an initial consonant, a vowel, and sometimes a final consonant written at the bottom. This final consonant is called 받침 [batchim]. Out of the 19 consonants you've learned, 16 can be used as 받침—excluding ㄸ, ㅉ, and ㅃ. At the end of a syllable, these 16 consonants are pronounced as only 7 sounds: ㄱ, ㄴ, ㄷ, ㄹ, ㅁ, ㅂ, and ㅇ.

PRONUNCIATION GUIDE

Video 05 MP3 13

See which consonants belong to each of the 7 sound groups, then listen and repeat the pronunciation of syllables using 받침. Even though you'll see 16 different consonants as 받침, you're really just using the same 7 sounds again and again.

Sound Groups of Final Consonants

Sound Group	Final Consonants	Example
ㄱ [k]	ㄱ ㅋ ㄲ	악 앜 앆 ➡ [악 ak]
	Similar to the ending "k" in "book." Stop the sound with the back of your tongue lightly touching the roof of your mouth. Don't release extra air.	
ㄴ [n]	ㄴ	안 ➡ [안 an]
	A clear "n" sound, like in "man" or "sun." Let the tip of your tongue touch your upper gums and hold the sound briefly.	
ㄷ [t]	ㄷ ㅌ ㅅ ㅆ ㅈ ㅊ ㅎ	앋 앝 앗 았 앚 앛 앟 ➡ [앋 at]
	A soft "t" sound, like in "cat" or "dot." Stop the sound with your tongue on the roof of your mouth and don't let out any air.	
ㄹ [l]	ㄹ	알 ➡ [알 al]
	A soft "l" sound, similar to "ball" or "seal." Place the tip of your tongue on the roof of your mouth.	

Sound Group	Final Consonants	Example
ㅁ [m]	ㅁ	암 ➡ [암 am]
	A clear "m" sound, like in "calm" or "ham." Gently close your lips and keep the sound soft and nasal.	
ㅂ [p]	ㅂ ㅍ	압 앞 ➡ [압 ap]
	An unaspirated "p" sound, like in "cap" or "tip." Close your lips completely and end the sound without a burst of air.	
ㅇ [ng]	ㅇ	앙 ➡ [앙 ang]
	A nasal "ng" sound, like in "song" or "ring." Keep the back of your tongue touching the soft part of the roof of your mouth.	

☑ Self-Check

1. Circle the correct final consonant sound for each word.

(1) 밖: [ㄱ k] [ㄴ n] [ㄷ t] [ㄹ l] [ㅁ m] [ㅂ p] [ㅇ ng]

(2) 밭: [ㄱ k] [ㄴ n] [ㄷ t] [ㄹ l] [ㅁ m] [ㅂ p] [ㅇ ng]

(3) 옷: [ㄱ k] [ㄴ n] [ㄷ t] [ㄹ l] [ㅁ m] [ㅂ p] [ㅇ ng]

(4) 숲: [ㄱ k] [ㄴ n] [ㄷ t] [ㄹ l] [ㅁ m] [ㅂ p] [ㅇ ng]

(5) 빛: [ㄱ k] [ㄴ n] [ㄷ t] [ㄹ l] [ㅁ m] [ㅂ p] [ㅇ ng]

2. Find the one that is pronounced differently from the others.

(1) ① 압 ② 암 ③ 앞

(2) ① 강 ② 갓 ③ 갈

(3) ① 묵 ② 문 ③ 묵 ④ 묶

(4) ① 낮 ② 낯 ③ 남 ④ 낫

(5) ① 안 ② 알 ③ 앝 ④ 았

(6) ① 숟 ② 숯 ③ 숲 ④ 숱

3. Write the English letters that represent the sound inside [ ].

(1) 받침 [ba__-chi__]

(2) 한국 [ha__-gu__]

(3) 한글 [ha__-geu__]

(4) 공책 [go__-chae__]

[Answer Key] **1.** (1) [ㄱ k] (2) [ㄷ t] (3) [ㄷ t] (4) [ㅂ p] (5) [ㄷ t]
2. (1) ② (2) ① (3) ② (4) ③ (5) ② (6) ③
3. (1) t, m (2) n, k (3) n, l (4) ng, k

PRACTICE WRITING 받침

MP3 14

Practice writing one-syllable words with final consonants. Pay attention to how each final consonant is placed in the syllable block. The actual pronunciation is shown in [ ] in both Korean and English. Listen closely to the final sounds as you repeat them.

채 + ㄱ [책 chaek]

book

책

바 + ㄲ [박 bak]

outside

밖

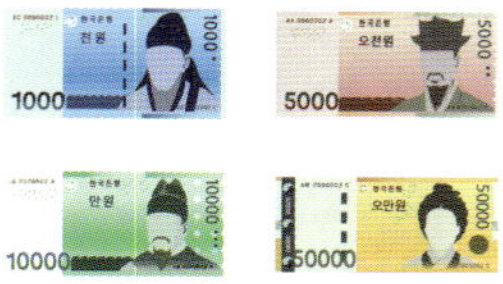

도 + ㄴ [돈 don]

money

돈

고 + ㅁ [곰 gom]

bear

곰

미 + ㅌ [믿 mit]

under, below

밑

나 + ㅈ [낟 nat]

daytime

낮

오 + ㅅ [옫 ot]

clothes

옷

꼬 + ㅊ [꼳 kkot]

flower

꽃

다 + ㄹ [달 dal]

moon

달

바 + ㅂ [밥 bap]

steamed rice, meal

밥

수 + ㅍ [숩 sup]

forest

숲

바 + ㅇ [방 bang]

room

방

WORDS WITH 받침

MP3 15

Try saying each word out loud, then trace the gray letters to practice writing the Korean characters yourself.

가족
[ga-jok]
family

엄마
[eom-ma]
mom

언니
[eon-ni]
older sister (for females)

동생
[dong-saeng]
younger sibling

사람
[sa-ram]
person

친구
[chin-gu]
friend

학생
[hak-saeng]
student

선생님
[seon-saeng-nim]
teacher

여행
[yeo-haeng]
travel, trip

택시
[taek-si]
taxi

식당
[sik-dang]
restaurant

공항
[gong-hang]
airport

먹다
[meok-da]
to eat

김치
[gim-chi]
kimchi

라면
[ra-myeon]
ramyeon, instant noodles

삼겹살
[sam-gyeop-sal]
samgyeopsal (pork belly)

Essential Practices

MP3 16

1. Listen carefully to the audio and circle the correct sound.

(1) 숲 순 숨

(2) 곧 곰 공

(3) 집 짐 징

(4) 밖 밥 밭

(5) 달 닻 단

(6) 낮 남 낙

(7) 책 챙 챗

(8) 꽃 꼰 꼭

2. Write down the words you hear and circle the correct picture.

(1) ☐  

(2) ☐   

(3) ☐  

(4) ☐☐  

(5) ☐☐  

(6) ☐☐☐  

3. Listen carefully and try writing the words in 한글. Use the picture as a hint!

(1) 치☐ 

(2) 오☐지 

(3) ☐고기 

(4) ☐퓨터 

One Step Forward!

Now that you've learned all the **한글** letters, you can write your name in Korean!
Try writing your name in **한글**. If your name ends with a consonant, you can add the vowel ㅡ [eu].
For example, Chris becomes **크리스**, and Dave becomes **데이브**.

나의 한글 이름 : ____________________
My Name in 한글

Call It by Its Name: How 한글 Letters Are Named

MP3 17

Just like each letter in the English alphabet has a name, every 한글 letter has its own name too. What's interesting is that there's a clear pattern behind how these names are formed.

For vowels, the name matches the sound, so you've already learned them.

For consonants, each name usually has two syllables: the first combines the consonant with ㅣ, and the second adds 으 with the consonant as a 받침 (final sound). The image below shows where the consonant fits into this pattern.

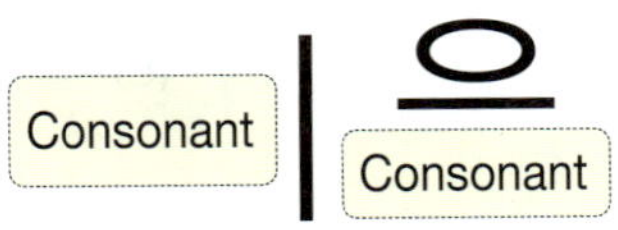

There are a few exceptions—ㄱ (기역), ㄷ (디귿), and ㅅ (시옷)—which have slight changes to make them easier to say. Tense consonants like ㄲ or ㄸ use the prefix 쌍 (pair), to show that the consonant is doubled.

Try picking letters at random and saying their names—it's a fun way to practice your pronunciation!

ㅏ 아 a	ㅐ 애 ae	ㅑ 야 ya	ㅒ 얘 yae	ㅓ 어 eo	ㅔ 에 e	ㅕ 여 yeo
ㅖ 예 ye	ㅗ 오 o	ㅘ 와 wa	ㅙ 왜 wae	ㅚ 외 oe	ㅛ 요 yo	ㅜ 우 u
ㅝ 워 weo	ㅞ 웨 we	ㅟ 위 wi	ㅠ 유 yu	ㅡ 으 eu	ㅢ 의 eui	ㅣ 이 i

ㄱ 기역 gi-yeok	ㄲ 쌍기역 ssang-gi-yeok	ㄴ 니은 ni-eun	ㄷ 디귿 di-geut	ㄸ 쌍디귿 ssang-di-geut	ㄹ 리을 ri-eul	ㅁ 미음 mi-eum
ㅂ 비읍 bi-eup	ㅃ 쌍비읍 ssang-bi-eup	ㅅ 시옷 si-ot	ㅆ 쌍시옷 ssang-si-ot	ㅇ 이응 i-eung	ㅈ 지읒 ji-eut	ㅉ 쌍지읒 ssang-ji-eut
ㅊ 치읓 chi-eut	ㅋ 키읔 ki-euk	ㅌ 티읕 ti-eut	ㅍ 피읖 pi-eup	ㅎ 히읗 hi-eut		

UNIT 7

The Final Touch: Pronunciation Tips 마무리 단계 : 발음 팁

한국어가 좋아요
[한구거] [조아요]

If you've made it this far, you can already read 99% of **한글**. Now let's go over a few tips to help you sound more natural. You don't need to memorize every rule—just say the words out loud when you see [ ]. These show the actual pronunciation in **한글**. The more you repeat them, the more natural they'll feel.

Video 06 MP3 18

DOUBLE FINAL CONSONANTS: ONLY ONE IS PRONOUNCED

Some syllables have two consonants in the **받침** (final consonant) position, but usually only the first one is pronounced. If the next syllable starts with a consonant, that consonant is pronounced more strongly—almost like a double sound. For example, **앉다** is pronounced [안따], not [안다].

Double Final Consonants [Sound]	ㄱㅅ [ㄱ]	ㄹㅂ [ㄹ]	ㅂㅅ [ㅂ]	ㄴㅈ [ㄴ]	ㄹㄱ [ㄱ]
Words					
	몫	여덟	값	앉다	흙
	[목]	[여덜]	[갑]	[안따]	[흑]
	share, portion	eight	price, value	to sit	soil, dirt

☑ Self-Check

1. Circle the final consonant that is pronounced and read the word aloud.

(1) 닭 (2) 앉다 (3) 읽다 (4) 짧다 (5) 삯 (6) 없다

2. Circle the correct pronunciation for the following words.

(1) 앉다: [안다] [안따] [안따] (2) 넓다: [널다] [넙따] [널따] (3) 읽다: [일다] [일따] [익따]

[Answer Key] 1. (1) ㄱ (pronunciation: 닥) (2) ㄴ (pronunciation: 안따) (3) ㄱ (pronunciation: 익따) (4) ㄹ (pronunciation: 짤따) (5) ㄱ (pronunciation: 삭) (6) ㅂ (pronunciation: 업따)
2. (1) [안따] (2) [널따] (3) [익따]

LIAISON (LINKING SOUND)

MP3 19

When a 받침 (final consonant) is followed by a vowel, it "moves over" and is pronounced at the beginning of the next syllable.

If a syllable has a double final consonant, the first consonant stays as the 받침, and the second one moves to the next syllable with the vowel.

However, when the 받침 is ㅇ [ng], it does not shift over; instead, it remains in its original position and retains its sound.

한국어	있어요	읽어요	종이
[한구거]	[이써요]	[일거요]	[종이]
The final ㄱ of 국 links to the following vowel sound.	The final ㅆ of 있 links to the following vowel sound.	The final ㅈ of 앉 links to the following vowel sound.	The final ㅇ of 종 does not move; it remains as [ng].

This rule is especially important because many common markers (particles) in Korean—like 은, 이, 을, and 에—start with vowels. Since they're used all the time, this rule helps you speak more naturally.

☑ Self-Check

1. Inside the brackets [ ], write the Korean characters as they sound.

(1) 음악 [으막]　　(2) 밥을 [ ]

(3) 돈이 [ ]　　(4) 옷을 [ ]

(5) 앉아요 [ ]　　(6) 공이 [ ]

(7) 사람이 [ ]　　(8) 영어 [ ]

(9) 숲은 [ ]　　(10) 공항에 [ ]

(11) 꽃이 [ ]　　(12) 독일인 [ ]

[Answer Key] **1.** (1) [으막] (2) [바블] (3) [도니] (4) [오슬] (5) [안자요] (6) [공이] (7) [사라미] (8) [영어] (9) [수픈] (10) [공항에] (11) [꼬치] (12) [도기린]

PRONUNCIATION RULES FOR ㅎ

MP3 20

- **Aspirated Variations:** When ㄱ, ㄷ, ㅂ, or ㅈ are combined with ㅎ, they change into their aspirated versions: ㅋ, ㅌ, ㅍ, and ㅊ.

Change with ㅎ	ㄱ + ㅎ → [ㅋ]	ㄷ + ㅎ → [ㅌ]	ㅂ + ㅎ → [ㅍ]	ㅈ + ㅎ → [ㅊ]
Words	좋고 [조코]	좋다 [조타]	급히 [그피]	젖히다 [저치다]

- **Silent ㅎ:** When ㅎ is the final consonant and the next syllable starts with a vowel, ㅎ becomes silent and is not pronounced.

좋아요
[조아요]

This rule also applies when ㅎ is part of a double final consonant. For example, look at the word 많다 (to be many/much) and how its different forms are pronounced.

많다	많지	많고	많아요
[만타]	[만치]	[만코]	[마나요]
ㅎ + ㄷ → [ㅌ]	ㅎ + ㅈ → [ㅊ]	ㅎ + ㄱ → [ㅋ]	ㅎ + vowel → Ø

☑ Self-Check

1. Inside the brackets [ ], write the Korean characters as they sound.

(1) 놓다 [노타]
(2) 급해요 [ ]
(3) 똑똑하다 [ ]
(4) 파랗고 [ ]
(5) 좋아요 [ ]
(6) 박하 [ ]
(7) 닿지 [ ]
(8) 축하 [ ]

2. ㅎ rule applies when ㅎ is part of a double final consonant. Inside the brackets [ ], write the Korean characters as they sound.

(1) 싫다 [실타] 싫고 [ ] 싫어요 [ ] 싫지 [ ]
(2) 괜찮다 [ ] 괜찮고 [ ] 괜찮아요 [ ] 괜찮지 [ ]

[Answer Key] **1.** (1) [노타] (2) [그패요] (3) [똑또카다] (4) [파라코] (5) [조아요] (6) [바카] (7) [다치] (8) [추카]
2. (1) [실타], [실코], [시러요], [실치] (2) [괜찬타], [괜찬코], [괜차나요], [괜찬치]

ADDITIONAL PRONUNCIATION RULES

MP3 21

Sometimes, Korean sounds change slightly to make pronunciation smoother. Below are some helpful rules.

Palatalization

Palatalization is when a sound shifts closer to the roof of your mouth. This happens when ㄷ or ㅌ comes before 이 or 히, making them sound like ㅈ or ㅊ.

final ㄷ + 이 → [지]	final ㅌ + 이 → [치]	final ㄷ + 히 → [치]
굳이 [구지]	같이 [가치]	닫히다 [다치다]

Nasalization

Nasalization is when a sound becomes nasal, like m, n, or ng. It occurs when the final consonant sounds [ㅂ], [ㄷ], or [ㄱ] are followed by ㅁ or ㄴ. The sound then changes to ㅁ, ㄴ, or ㅇ to match the nasal sound.

[ㅂ] + ㄴ → [ㅁ] + ㄴ	[ㄷ] + ㄴ → [ㄴ] + ㄴ	[ㄱ] + ㄴ → [ㅇ] + ㄴ
감사합니다 [감사함니다]	걷는 [건는]	작년 [장년]

[ㅂ] + ㅁ → [ㅁ] + ㅁ	[ㄷ] + ㅁ → [ㄴ] + ㅁ	[ㄱ] + ㅁ → [ㅇ] + ㅁ
밥맛 [밤맏]	콧물 [콘물]	박물관 [방물관]

UNIT 8

Greetings and Responses

인사말과 응답 표현

한글 unlocked! Now it's time to start speaking. Let's start with some of the most common Korean greetings and basic responses. Think about the situations where these phrases are used and say them out loud several times.

ANSWERS TO QUESTIONS

MP3 22

Yes.
네.

No.
아니요.

In casual speech (반말), you can use 응 or 어 for "Yes," and 아니 for "No."

BASIC GREETINGS AND RESPONSES

MP3 23

Hello!
안녕하세요.

You may also see **안녕하세요?** with a question mark because it literally means "Are you at peace?" or "Are you doing well?". It looks like a question, but it functions as a greeting.

(when answering the phone) Hello?
여보세요.

When answering or starting a phone call, you say **여보세요** instead of **안녕하세요**.

Nice to meet you.

(만나서) 반갑습니다. / 반가워요.

[반갑씀니다]

반갑습니다 is commonly used when meeting someone for the first time. It is also frequently used in semi-formal situations. The less formal version is 반가워요, which is suitable for more casual interactions.

Thank you.

감사합니다. / 고맙습니다.

[감사함니다] [고맙씀니다]

You might also have heard of 고마워요 as a way to say "Thank you." However, be cautious with 고마워요, as it is appropriate only with people of lower status, younger individuals, or close friends.

I am sorry. / Excuse me.

죄송합니다. / 죄송해요.

[죄송함니다]

You might also have heard of 미안합니다/미안해요, which is generally used with friends or younger people.

No, it is not. / You're welcome.

아니에요.

The phrase 아니에요 literally means "It's not" or "Not at all," and is used to deny or correct a statement. In everyday conversation, it's also often used in response to 감사합니다/고맙습니다 or 죄송합니다/죄송해요— similar to saying "You're welcome" or "No problem."

It's okay. / I'm fine. / No, thank you.

괜찮습니다. / 괜찮아요.

[괜찬씀니다] [괜차나요]

괜찮습니다/괜찮아요 is a versatile phrase in Korean that can mean "It's okay," "I'm fine," or "No, thank you," depending on the context. It is often used to reassure someone after an apology, describe one's physical or emotional state, or politely decline an offer.

☑ Self-Check

1. Match the English meanings with the Korean phrases.

(1) 네.	•	• ① Hello! / Hi!
(2) 아니요.	•	• ② No.
(3) 안녕하세요.	•	• ③ Thank you.
(4) 여보세요.	•	• ④ (on the phone) Hello?
(5) 반갑습니다./반가워요.	•	• ⑤ I am sorry. / Excuse me.
(6) 감사합니다./고맙습니다.	•	• ⑥ It's okay. / I'm fine. / No, thank you.
(7) 아니에요.	•	• ⑦ No, it is not. / You're welcome.
(8) 죄송합니다./죄송해요.	•	• ⑧ Nice to meet you.
(9) 괜찮습니다./괜찮아요.	•	• ⑨ Yes.

2. Check the following situations and choose the most appropriate expression from the options provided.

안녕하세요　　감사합니다　　죄송합니다　　괜찮아요　　반갑습니다

(1) You are walking down the street and see your coworker, 김민수 씨. How would you greet them?

You: ________________, 민수 씨!

(2) You've just met someone for the first time and exchanged names. How would you express that you're pleased to meet them?

You: ________________.

(3) You dropped something on the street, and a stranger picked it up for you. What would you say to them?

You: ________________.

(4) You're walking through a crowded subway station, and you accidentally brush against someone's arm. How would this conversation likely go?

You: 아, ________________!

Stranger: ________________.

[Answer Key] 1. (1) ⑨ (2) ② (3) ① (4) ④ (5) ⑧ (6) ③ (7) ⑦ (8) ⑤ (9) ⑥
2. (1) 안녕하세요 (2) 반갑습니다 (3) 감사합니다 (4) 죄송합니다, 괜찮아요

AT THE TABLE

MP3 24

Enjoy your meal!

맛있게 드세요.

[마싣께 드세요]

When sharing a meal, it's common to say 맛있게 드세요 to each other. Restaurant staff also say this when serving your food.

(starting eating) Thank you for the meal.

잘 먹겠습니다.

[잘 먹껟씀니다]

To directly translate, this phrase means "I will eat well" and is commonly said before starting a meal as a way to express gratitude, often directed at the host, cook, or anyone present.

(after eating) Thank you for the meal.

잘 먹었습니다.

[잘 머걷씀니다]

To directly translate, this phrase means "I ate well" and is said after finishing a meal to show gratitude. It's a polite way to thank the host or cook for the food, acknowledging their effort. It also reflects satisfaction with the meal.

TO SAY GOODBYE

MP3 25

Goodbye!

안녕히 가세요.

Farewells depend on who is leaving. If both are leaving, they say 안녕히 가세요 to each other. If one stays and the other leaves, the person leaving says 안녕히 계세요 to the one staying, while the person staying says 안녕히 가세요 to the leaver.

Goodbye! (Stay in peace.)

안녕히 계세요.

To directly translate, 안녕히 계세요 means "Stay in peace" and is used when you are leaving and the other person is staying behind.

☑ Self-Check

1. Match the English meanings with the Korean phrases.

(1) 맛있게 드세요. •
(2) 잘 먹겠습니다. •
(3) 잘 먹었습니다. •
(4) 안녕히 가세요. •
(5) 안녕히 계세요. •

• ① (After eating) Thank you for the meal.
• ② (Leaver → Stayer) Stay in peace!
• ③ (Stayer → Leaver) Goodbye!
• ④ (Starting eating) Thank you for the meal.
• ⑤ Enjoy your meal!

2. Alex invites you over and serves you some delicious 김밥. Read each situation and choose the most appropriate expression.

안녕히 계세요 　 잘 먹겠습니다 　 맛있게 드세요 　 아니에요
안녕히 가세요 　 잘 먹었습니다

(1) Alex brings the 김밥 to the table with a big smile and says this to you: ____________________!

(2) The 김밥 looks delicious! As you start eating, you would say: ____________________!

(3) You've finished the delicious 김밥. You would express your gratitude after the meal like:
____

(4) The 김밥 was so good! You thank Alex for making it. How would Alex humbly respond?

You: 김밥 고마워요, 알렉스 씨! Thank you for the 김밥, Alex!

Alex: ____________________.

(5) After enjoying the meal and spending time together, it's time to leave Alex's house. How would you both say goodbye?

Alex: ____________________!

You: ____________________, 알렉스 씨!

[Answer Key] 1. (1) ⑤ (2) ④ (3) ① (4) ③ (5) ②
2. (1) 맛있게 드세요 (2) 잘 먹겠습니다 (3) 잘 먹었습니다 (4) 아니에요 (5) 안녕히 가세요, 안녕히 계세요

WRITING GREETINGS AND RESPONSES

Let's read the greetings and responses out loud and try writing them as we go.

1 Answers to Questions

네. Yes.	네.	
아니요. No.	아니요.	

2 Basic Greetings and Responses

안녕하세요. Hello!	안녕하세요.	
여보세요. (on the phone) Hello?	여보세요.	
(만나서) 반갑습니다. Nice to meet you.	반갑습니다.	
(만나서) 반가워요. Nice to meet you.	반가워요.	
감사합니다. Thank you.	감사합니다.	
고맙습니다. Thank you.	고맙습니다.	
죄송합니다. I am sorry. / Excuse me.	죄송합니다.	
죄송해요. I am sorry. / Excuse me.	죄송해요.	

아니에요. No, it is not. / You're welcome.	아니에요.	
괜찮습니다. It's okay. / I'm fine. / No, thank you.	괜찮습니다.	
괜찮아요. It's okay. / I'm fine. / No, thank you.	괜찮아요.	

3 At the Table

맛있게 드세요. Enjoy your meal!	맛있게 드세요.	
잘 먹겠습니다. (starting eating) Thank you for the meal.	잘 먹겠습니다.	
잘 먹었습니다. (after eating) Thank you for the meal.	잘 먹었습니다.	

4 To Say Goodbye

안녕히 가세요. (to the leaver) Goodbye!	안녕히 가세요.	
안녕히 계세요. (to the stayer) Goodbye!	안녕히 계세요.	

PART 2

Essential Patterns

Congratulations on completing 한글 part! Now it's time to learn key Korean phrases and grammar to develop practical language skills. We'll start with core features of Korean, helping you understand how it differs from English.

Many grammar patterns include nouns or the stems of verbs and adjectives. Before we begin, remember that **N** stands for nouns, **A** for adjective stems, and **V** for verb stems. As you study, you will also come across commonly used irregular forms, which are indicated with an asterisk (*) mark. These irregular forms appear frequently in everyday speech, so it's helpful to memorize them as complete expressions.

This part is all about making your studies practical and enjoyable. Take it step by step, and you'll get closer to fluency with every sentence you learn. And here's the golden rule: practice out loud. You can also try writing directly over any gray Korean words you see.

UNIT 1

Key Features of Korean Language 한국어의 주요 특징

Video 07

We emphasize the importance of using Korean right from the beginning, instead of waiting to master every aspect of grammar and vocabulary. To help you get started, we highlight key features of the Korean language. These features not only make Korean easier to speak but also give you insight into its rich linguistic structure and cultural nuances.

LINGUISTIC FEATURES

1 S-O-V Structure

Unlike English, Korean places the predicate at the end of the sentence. The predicate, which can usually be a verb or an adjective (descriptive verb), expresses what is said about the subject. Because of this, Korean sentences typically follow a Subject-Object-Verb (S-O-V) structure.

리사 Lisa **피자** pizza **먹어요** eats

One great feature of Korean grammar is that the structure of questions and statements is the same—just change your tone!

- **Statement:** 리사 피자 먹어요. ↘ Lisa eats pizza.
- **Question:** 리사 피자 먹어요? ↗ Does Lisa eat pizza?

2 Markers (Particles)

Korean uses markers, or particles, to indicate grammatical roles of words such as subjects, objects, topics, or locations, rather than relying on word order. These short words—such as 이/가, 은/는, 을/를, 에, and many others—are **attached directly to words** like nouns without a space, specifying their grammatical function.

한국은
as the topic

한국이
as the subject

한국을
as the object

한국에
as the location

Thanks to these markers, Korean word order is quite flexible, allowing you to focus more on expressing your ideas rather than strictly following a fixed sentence structure.

3 Stems and Endings

Korean is an agglutinative language, which means that grammar is expressed through endings. There's a Korean saying: "Listen to Korean to the very end," because sentence endings contain essential information such as mood, tense, politeness, formality, and sentence type.

In their basic form, verbs and adjectives end with -다 (e.g., 먹다 = to eat). This is also called the dictionary form or infinitive form. To use these words in sentences, simply remove -다 at the end to get the stem, then attach different endings:

먹**다** to eat
└→ verb stem: 먹-

먹**어** eat (present, casual, informal)

먹**어요** eat (present, polite, informal)

먹**습니다** eat (present, polite, formal)

먹**었어** ate (past, casual, informal)

먹**었어요** ate (past, polite, informal)

먹**을 거예요** will eat (future, polite, informal)

먹**고 싶습니다** want to eat (present, polite, formal)

Korean also uses **connective endings** to link sentences, like "and" or "but" in English:

먹**고** eat and...

먹**지만** eat but...

먹**어서** because I eat...

All in all, endings play a key role in determining the meaning and tone of a sentence. The various grammar patterns you will learn are combinations of these endings.

④ Relying on Context: Omitting Elements in Sentences

In English, even if it's clear from the context who or what the sentence refers to, sentences still require certain elements like a subject or object to be explicitly stated. In contrast, Korean relies heavily on context to convey meaning, allowing you to omit these elements when they're already clear. For instance, when asking a friend if they like **김밥**, you might simply say **김밥 좋아해요?** ((Do you) like gimbap?). The subject "you" is left out because it's obvious from the situation. Also, you can respond **좋아해요!** ((I) like (it)!), leaving the object unstated since it's already clear from the question. This reliance on context means that you don't need to form perfectly complete sentences every time you speak. As long as you know the key words—like the action or description—you'll still be understood. So, relax, focus on the essentials, and enjoy expressing yourself in Korean with confidence!

☑ Self-Check

1. Circle the correct answer from the descriptions below.

(1) Korean sentences follow the structure of: [S-O-V / S-V-O / O-S-V].

(2) The subject of a Korean sentence [must always / does not have to] be stated explicitly.

(3) [Markers / Endings] are short words like 이/가, 은/는, 을/를, or 에 that indicate the grammatical role of a word.

(4) [Basic form / Stem] refers to the dictionary form of a verb or adjective, ending with -다.

(5) The essential information of a sentence, such as sentence type, mood, tense, politeness, and formality, is indicated by [endings / word order].

2. Underline the stem part of the following verbs or adjectives in their basic form.

(1) 먹다　(2) 좋아하다　(3) 맛있다　(4) 싸다　(5) 앉다　(6) 읽다

[Answer Key] 1. (1) S-O-V (2) does not have to (3) Markers (4) Basic form (5) endings
2. (1) 먹 (2) 좋아하 (3) 맛있 (4) 싸 (5) 앉 (6) 읽

CULTURAL FEATURES

1 Speech Styles and Honorifics

Respect is a fundamental part of Korean culture and is reflected in speech styles and honorifics. Factors such as age, social status, and familiarity with the listener strongly influence the way you address someone.

Korean speech styles are mainly divided into **존댓말** (polite speech) and **반말** (casual speech). **존댓말** is generally used when speaking to someone older than you, someone of higher rank, or someone you're not familiar with. Even when speaking to someone of the same age or younger, it is common to use **존댓말** unless you share a close relationship. **반말**, on the other hand, is reserved for close friends, peers, or younger people and should only be used when both parties agree. Speaking too casually without mutual consent may be perceived as rude.

The most noticeable difference between **존댓말** and **반말** lies in their sentence endings, often referred to as "ending styles." The **-습니다 ending style** is the most formal form of **존댓말**, recognizable by its **-니다** ending. It is typically used in professional or official settings, such as business meetings, presentations, or formal events. The **-해요 ending style**, a less formal version of **존댓말**, ends in **-요** and is widely used in daily conversations. Finally, the **-해** ending style is associated with **반말** and is used in casual speech. This style is often formed by removing **요** from the **-해요 ending style**, creating a tone that is more direct and informal.

in business meetings

between friends 존댓말 / 반말

Additionally, **존댓말** includes not only different ending styles but also honorifics (**높임말**), which involve changes in word choice or verb/adjective forms to show deference to the listener or the subject of the sentence. For example, the casual pronoun **나** (I) becomes **저** (I) when speaking politely. Similarly, verbs can be adjusted to include honorifics, such as **드리다** (to give in the humble form) instead of **주다** (to give).

We're primarily focusing on the **-해요 ending style** in this book. Starting with the versatile **-해요 ending style** will provide a strong foundation for speaking Korean naturally.

2 Indirect Expressions

In Korean, indirect expressions are often considered more natural. For example, instead of asking directly 이름이 뭐예요? (What is your name?), a more polite phrasing would be 이름이 어떻게 되세요? (How may I ask your name?).

Similarly, rather than directly stating "It is...," Koreans often say ~ 것 같아요 (It seems to be…). While ~ 것 같아요 originally conveys uncertainty, it is also widely used to soften statements when sharing feelings, giving feedback, or politely declining a request. These expressions allow speakers to communicate more gently, fostering smoother and more harmonious interactions. For instance, consider the question 토요일에 만날까요? (Shall we meet on Saturday?). A direct response like 아니요, 바빠요. (No, I'm busy that day.) might come across as blunt or firm. In contrast, a more indirect response like 미안해요. 그날 바쁠 것 같아요. (Sorry, I think I'll be busy that day.) is usually preferred in everyday conversations.

3 Proper Etiquette for Names and Titles

In Korean, people are typically addressed by their names or titles rather than pronouns like "he (그)" or "she (그녀)." When speaking directly to someone, we often omit the subject entirely or use the person's name or title instead of saying "you (당신/너)." Names are structured with the family name first, followed by the given name, written together without a space (e.g., 김민수). Family names are usually one syllable, while given names are typically two syllables.

How you address someone depends on formality and relationship. Adding 씨 to a name (e.g., 김민수 씨) is polite in everyday situations, while 님 (e.g., 김민수 님) shows more respect. Titles such as 선생님 (teacher) are used to address someone politely. A title can also be used with a name, like 김민수 선생님 or 김 선생님.

4 Sino-Korean Words

A significant portion of Korean vocabulary comes from Sino-Korean words (한자어), which are based on Chinese characters (한자). These words often appear in everyday conversations. For example, the Chinese character 학 (學), meaning "learning," is found in words like 학교 (school) and 학생 (student). Recognizing these roots can help you guess meanings and grow your vocabulary more easily. If the same character shows up in several similar words, it may be a Sino-Korean root. Spotting these patterns can give you a deeper understanding and help you remember words better.

☑ Self-Check

1. Write O for true and X for false.

(1) Korean no longer uses Chinese-character-based words. (   )

(2) You can always use 반말 (casual speech) with people of the same age. (   )

(3) In the Korean name 박지수, the family name is 박, and the given name is 지수. (   )

(4) The word for "I," 나, becomes 저 when speaking politely. (   )

(5) In Korean, direct expressions are preferred over indirect ones to sound polite. (   )

2. Fill in the blank with the correct term from the options below.

-습니다 ending style   -해요 ending style   씨   honorifics   반말

(1) ____________ is a casual speech style, typically used with close friends, peers, or younger people. It should only be used when both parties agree.

(2) ____________ is the most formal form of 존댓말 (polite speech), typically used in professional or official settings.

(3) ____________ is a less formal version of 존댓말 (polite speech) and is widely used in daily conversations.

(4) ____________ involve respectful word choices or verb/adjective changes as part of 존댓말.

(5) In Korean, adding ____________ after someone's name is a polite way to address them.

[Answer Key] **1.** (1) X (2) X (3) O (4) O (5) X
2. (1) 반말 (2) -습니다 ending style (3) -해요 ending style (4) honorifics (5) 씨

UNIT 2

Basic Markers

기본 조사

Video 08

Markers, or particles, attach to words to show their grammatical roles in a sentence. While the technical term is "postpositional particle," we'll simply call them markers, as they "mark" these roles. In this unit, we'll focus on three basic markers: the subject marker 이/가, the object marker 을/를, and the topic marker 은/는.

1 Review: S-O-V Structure

Before exploring markers, let's review the S-O-V (Subject-Object-Verb) structure, which means that the subject comes first, followed by the object (if any), and then the verb.

Try creating sentences using the provided words.

Nouns	**제니** Jennie **리암** Liam **날씨** weather **이 식당** this restaurant **케이크** cake **책** book
Verbs/Adjectives (with present tense ending)	**읽어요** read(s) [일거요] **좋아요** is fine [조아요] **비싸요** is expensive **먹어요** eat(s)

(1) Jennie reads a book. → 제니 책 읽어요.

(2) Liam eats cake. → ________ ________ ________

(3) The weather is fine. → ________ ________

(4) This restaurant is expensive. → ________ ________

According to the S-O-V structure, the sentences become:

(1) 제니 책 읽어요. (2) 리암 케이크 먹어요.

(3) 날씨 좋아요. (4) 이 식당 비싸요.

As you can see here, the verb/adjective (or predicate) always comes at the end of the sentence.

The same S-O-V structure applies to questions. When you speak, simply raise your tone at the end.

(1) 제니 책 읽어요.↘ → 제니 책 읽어요?↗

(2) 리암 케이크 먹어요.↘ → 리암 케이크 먹어요?↗

(3) 날씨 좋아요.↘ → 날씨 좋아요?↗

(4) 이 식당 비싸요.↘ → 이 식당 비싸요?↗

Adverbs can usually be placed almost anywhere, but they are often placed before the object or the predicate. When setting the overall context, such as time or place, adverbs are typically placed at the beginning of the sentence.

- **오늘 (Today)** **오늘** 날씨 좋아요. / 날씨 **오늘** 좋아요. (○)
- **지금 (Now)** **지금** 제니 책 읽어요. / 제니 **지금** 책 읽어요. (○)

2 Subject 이/가

The marker 이/가 marks the subject of a sentence—the one doing the action or being described. Attach 이 if the subject word ends with a consonant (받침) and 가 if it ends with a vowel (no 받침).

돈 + **이**
consonant
(받침 ○)

날씨 + **가**
vowel
(받침 ×)

Let's practice adding the correct subject marker (이 or 가) to the following sentences:

(1) 제니_____ 책 읽어요. Jennie reads a book.

(2) 리암_____ 케이크 먹어요. Liam eats cake.

(3) 날씨_____ 좋아요. The weather is fine.

(4) 이 식당_____ 비싸요. This restaurant is expensive.

After adding the subject marker, the sentences become:

(1) 제니가 책 읽어요.

(2) 리암이 케이크 먹어요.

(3) 날씨가 좋아요.

(4) 이 식당이 비싸요.

When you read the sentences aloud, pay attention to how the subject marker 이 connects with the consonant before it to create a smooth linking sound. In sentence (2), 리암이 is pronounced smoothly as [리아미].

When the subject is "I," 나 (casual "I") and 저 (polite "I") change to 내가 and 제가 when attaching 이/가.

나
casual
내가

저
polite
제가

3 Object 을/를

The marker 을/를 marks the direct object of a verb—the word receiving the action. Attach 을 if the object word ends with a consonant (받침) and 를 if it ends with a vowel (no 받침).

밥 + 을 — consonant (받침 ○)
한국어 + 를 — vowel (받침 ×)

Let's practice adding the correct object marker (을 or 를) to the following sentences:

(1) **한국어_____ 공부해요.** I study Korean.

(2) **꽃_____ 사요.** I buy flowers.

(3) **제니가 책_____ 읽어요.** Jennie reads a book.

(4) **리암이 케이크_____ 먹어요.** Liam eats cake.

After adding the object marker, the sentences become:

(1) 한국어**를** 공부해요.

(2) 꽃**을** 사요.

(3) 제니가 책**을** 읽어요.

(4) 리암이 케이크**를** 먹어요.

When you read the sentences aloud, pay attention to how the object marker 을 connects with the consonant before it, creating a smooth linking sound. For example, in sentence (2), 꽃을 is pronounced as [꼬츨]. In sentence (3), 책을 is pronounced as [채글].

In Korean, object markers are often omitted in casual conversation. For example, instead of 한국어를 공부해요, you might hear 한국어 공부해요. And instead of 책을 읽어요, people often say 책 읽어요.

4 Topic 은/는

The marker 은/는 marks the topic of a sentence, indicating what the sentence is mainly about. While "topic" might sound quite grand, 은/는 simply marks the main focus. You'll frequently use 은/는 when starting a conversation or constructing simple sentences.

Attach 은 if the topic word ends with a consonant (받침), and 는 if it ends with a vowel (no 받침).

오늘 + 은 — consonant (받침 ○)

저 + 는 — vowel (받침 ×)

Let's practice adding the correct topic marker (은 or 는) to the following sentences:

(1) **저_____ 책을 읽어요.** I read a book.

(2) **리암_____ 케이크를 먹어요.** Liam eats cake.

(3) **이 식당_____ 비싸요.** This restaurant is expensive.

(4) **오늘_____ 날씨가 좋아요.** The weather is fine today.

(5) **지금_____ 제가 바빠요.** I am busy now.

After adding the topic marker, the sentences become:

(1) 저**는** 책을 읽어요.

(2) 리암**은** 케이크를 먹어요.

(3) 이 식당**은** 비싸요.

(4) 오늘**은** 날씨가 좋아요.

(5) 지금**은** 제가 바빠요.

As seen in sentences (4) and (5), 은/는 is not limited to the subject of a sentence. 은/는 can also be attached to other parts, like adverbs, to set the topic and highlight what the speaker wants to focus on.

When reading the sentences aloud, notice how 은 combines with the final consonant of the preceding word to create a smooth linking sound. For example, in sentence (2), 리암은 is pronounced as [리아믄].

EXPLORE FURTHER

When to Use 은/는 or 이/가 for the Subject?

You might wonder how 은/는 is different from 이/가. Simply put, 은/는 sets the topic of the sentence ("as for N"), while 이/가 points out or emphasizes the subject.

제가 한국어를 공부해요: Focus on "I" as the one studying Korean.
저는 한국어를 공부해요: Focus on "I" as the topic, showing what I'm doing.

If you're unsure, 은/는 is usually a safe choice, especially when starting a new sentence.

Essential Practices

MP3 26

1. Match the markers to the correct type of word.

(1) 이 • — • subject

(2) 은 •

(3) 를 • — • object

(4) 가 •

(5) 을 • — • topic

(6) 는 •

2. Circle the correct marker for each sentence.

(1) 시계(이/가) 비싸요. The clock is expensive.

(2) 치킨(이/가) 맛있어요. The chicken is delicious.

(3) 이 바지(은/는) 싸요. These pants are cheap.

(4) 밥(을/를) 먹어요. I eat a meal.

(5) 여행(을/를) 좋아해요. I like traveling.

(6) 미국(은/는) 날씨(이/가) 추워요. As for the U.S., the weather is cold.

(7) 호주(은/는) 날씨(이/가) 더워요. As for Australia, the weather is hot.

(8) 크리스 씨(은/는) 한국 영화(을/를) 좋아해요. Chris likes Korean movies.

(9) 김 선생님(은/는) 한국어(을/를) 가르쳐요. Mr. Kim teaches Korean.

(10) 저(은/는) 지금 돈(이/가) 없어요. I don't have money now.

3. Fill in the blanks with the correct marker. Use each marker only once to match the English sentences.

은	는	이	가	을	를

(1) **I** study Korean. → 제___ 한국어를 공부해요.

(2) **Yesterday**, I ate pizza. → 어제___ 피자를 먹었어요.

(3) Liam drinks **milk**. → 리암이 우유___ 마셔요.

(4) **For now**, I don't have money. → 지금___ 돈이 없어요.

(5) Lisa eats **ramyeon**. → 리사는 라면___ 먹어요.

(6) As for this restaurant, the **bibimbap** is delicious. → 이 식당은 비빔밥___ 맛있어요.

UNIT 3

Demonstrative Pronouns 이/그/저 지시 대명사 이/그/저

In English, we use "this" and "that" before nouns to indicate which object or person we are referring to. Korean also has similar words that function the same way. 이, 그, and 저 are demonstrative pronouns used to refer to things or people based on their distance from the speaker and listener.

1 Understanding 이/그/저 Through Distance

이, 그, and 저 come before the noun they describe, just like "this" and "that" in English. 이 (this) is used when something is close to the speaker. 그 (that) is used when something is close to the listener. 저 (that over there) is used when something is far from both the speaker and the listener.

이 this	그 that	저 that over there
close to the speaker	close to the listener	far from both speaker & listener

2 Using 이/그/저 with Nouns

Just like "this" and "that" in English, you can place 이/그/저 before nouns to indicate which person, place, or thing you are referring to. Look at the image below and fill in the speech bubbles with 이, 그, or 저.

The correct answers in order are 이, 그, 저.

If you use the name of a noun, you can simply attach 이, 그, or 저 in front of it. However, in daily conversations, when referring to people, places, or certain things, there are a few extra points to keep in mind.

1 Referring to People: 이/그/저 + 사람/분

When talking about people, simply attach 이/그/저 to 사람 (person): 이 사람, 그 사람, and 저 사람.

When referring to someone older, in a higher position, or unknown to the speaker, use 분, the honorific form of 사람. This shows respect for the person you're talking about: 이분 (this person), 그분 (that person), and 저분 (that person over there). 이분, 그분, and 저분 are written as one word without a space.

이 사람 this person	**이분** this person (honorific)
그 사람 that person	**그분** that person (honorific)
저 사람 that person over there	**저분** that person over there (honorific)

2 Referring to Places: 이/그/저 + 곳

When talking about places, use 이곳 (this place), 그곳 (that place), and 저곳 (that place over there). The word 곳 means "place," and these forms are written as one word without a space.

There are common alternatives for everyday conversation: 여기 (here), 거기 (there) and 저기 (over there).

이곳 = 여기 this place, here	**그곳 = 거기** that place, there	**저곳 = 저기** that place over there, over there

3 Referring to Things: 이/그/저 + 것

When referring to things, you can use 이것 (this thing), 그것 (that thing), and 저것 (that thing over there). The word 것 means "thing" and is often used in a general sense. 이것, 그것, and 저것 are written as one word without a space.

In spoken Korean, they are often shortened for easier pronunciation: 이거, 그거, and 저거.

이것 ➡ 이거 this thing	**그것 ➡ 그거** that thing	**저것 ➡ 저거** that thing over there

Since these forms are used frequently in conversation, they often combine with grammatical markers in a contracted form in spoken language.

이것/그것/저것 + 은/는 topic marker	이것/그것/저것 + 이/가 subject marker	이것/그것/저것 + 을/를 object marker
이것은 → 이건	이것이 → 이게	이것을 → 이걸
그것은 → 그건	그것이 → 그게	그것을 → 그걸
저것은 → 저건	저것이 → 저게	저것을 → 저걸

4 Referring to Something Mentioned in Context

이 and 그 can also refer to something already mentioned in conversation or text.

어제 카페에 갔어요. **거기**에 사람이 많았어요.
= 카페

Yesterday, I went to a café. A lot of people were **there**.
= café

어제 리사 씨를 만났어요. **그분**은 친절했어요.
= 리사 씨

Yesterday, I met Lisa. **That person** was kind.
= Lisa

Tip!

Sometimes 이 can be used for emphasis when referring to something just mentioned. Generally, 그 is used more often in both spoken and written Korean.

Essential Practices

MP3 27

1. Complete the table below based on what you have learned.

	이 this	그 that	저 that over there
Thing	이것, 이거	,	,
Person	,	,	저 사람, 저분
Place	,	그곳, 거기	,

2. Fill in the blanks to rewrite the sentences in a more natural and conversational way.

(1) 저것을 보세요! → ___저걸___ 보세요! Look at that (over there)!

(2) 이것이 뭐예요? → ________ 뭐예요? What is this?

(3) 그것은 책이에요. → ________ 책이에요. That is a book.

(4) 저것은 너무 커요. → ________ 너무 커요. That (over there) is too big.

(5) 그것을 주세요. → ________ 주세요. Please give me that thing.

3. Fill in the blanks with 이, 그, or 저 to match the English sentence.

(1) **This book** is fun. → ___이___ 책은 재미있어요.

(2) I got a letter. **The letter** was touching. → 편지를 받았어요. _____ 편지는 감동적이었어요.

(3) Who is **that person over there**? → _____ 사람이 누구예요?

(4) Lisa, how much is **that skirt** (you are holding)? → 리사 씨, _____ 치마 얼마예요?

(5) I read a book. **The book** was interesting. → 책을 읽었어요. _____ 책은 재미있었어요.

UNIT 4

N이/가 있어요/없어요

① There is/isn't N ② have/don't have N

Video 10

The pattern **N이/가 있어요** means "there is N" or "I have N," while **N이/가 없어요** means "there isn't N" or "I don't have N." The meaning depends on the context. For example, **돈이 있어요** can mean "There is money" when talking about a place, or "I have money" when talking about what you own. As you practice, think about whether the sentence is about existence or possession.

CRACKING THE PATTERN CODE

있어요 and **없어요** express both existence and possession with the subject markers **이/가**.

○ N 이/가 **있어요** [이써요]	× N 이/가 **없어요** [업써요]
① There **is/are** N.	① There **is/are not** N.
② I **have** N.	② I **don't have** N.

The basic form of **있어요** is **있다**, and the basic form of **없어요** is **없다**.

To talk about where something exists or doesn't exist, use the place marker **에** with a location noun.

(location)**에** N이/가 있어요/없어요

집에 고양이가 있어요. There's a cat at home.

고양이가 차에 없어요. There isn't a cat in the car.

돈 money • 집 home, house • 고양이 cat • 차 car • 선생님 teacher • 시간 time • 현금 cash

To mark who has something, the topic marker 은/는 is usually used for the possessor. (Sometimes, 이/가 can also be used to emphasize who has it.)

(topic)은/는 N이/가 있어요/없어요

선생님은 고양이가 있어요. The teacher has a cat.

저는 고양이가 없어요. I don't have a cat.

In spoken Korean, the subject marker 이/가 is often left out in the 있어요/없어요 pattern, especially in questions.

시간 있어요? Do you have time?

현금 없어요? Don't you have cash?

CORE SENTENCES

MP3 28

○ [Noun]이/가 있어요

오늘 수업이 있어요. I have a class today.

저는 언니가 있어요. I have an older sister.

마트에 과일이 있어요. There is fruit at the supermarket.

집에 우유가 있어요. There is milk at home.

× [Noun]이/가 없어요

오늘 약속이 없어요. I don't have an appointment today.

저는 오빠가 없어요. I don't have an older brother.

지갑에 현금이 없어요. There is no cash in the wallet.

여기에 카페가 없어요. There is no café here.

In casual speech, the subject marker 이/가 is often left out:

오렌지주스 있어요? Do you have orange juice?

내일 시간 있어요? Do you have time tomorrow?

Essential Practices

MP3 29

1. Write 있어요 or 없어요 to complete the sentence. Then, read it aloud.

(1) ◯ 저기에 카페가 ______________. There is a café over there.

(2) ✕ 시간이 ______________. I don't have time.

(3) ✕ 약속이 ______________. I don't have an appointment.

(4) ◯ 현금 ______________? Do you have cash?

(5) ◯ 커피 ______________? Do you have coffee (on the menu)?

2. Use the given word in the pattern and say it out loud.

(1) **편의점** convenience store ◯

→ 저기에 ___편의점이___ ___있어요___. There is a convenience store over there.

(2) **파스타** pasta ✕

→ 이 식당은 __________ __________. This restaurant has no pasta.

(3) **형** older brother (of males) ✕ **누나** older sister (of males) ◯

→ 민수 씨는 ___형이___ ___없어요___. ___누나가___ ___있어요___.

Minsu doesn't have an older brother. He has an older sister.

(4) **오빠** older brother (of females) ✕ **언니** older sister (of females) ◯

→ 하나 씨는 __________ __________. __________ __________.

Hana doesn't have an older brother. She has an older sister.

3. Use the hint words to complete the conversation. Then, practice reading it aloud.

(1) **시간** time, **약속** appointment

A: 내일 ___시간___ 있어요? Do you have time tomorrow?

B: 아니요, 내일 ___약속___ (이)/가 ___있어요___. No, I have an appointment tomorrow.

(2) **화장실** toilet, **저기** over there

A: __________ 이/가 어디에 __________? Where is the toilet?

B: __________ 에 있어요. It's over there.

(3) **오렌지주스** orange juice, **저희** we

A: __________ __________? Do you have orange juice (on the menu)?

B: 죄송해요. 저희는 __________ 이/가 __________. Sorry, we don't have orange juice.

UNIT 5

N이에요/예요

am/are/is N

Video 11

The pattern **N이에요/예요** works like "am/are/is N" in English. It is used to describe attributes such as a name, nationality, job, price, or other identifying details. You'll hear and use this pattern all the time in Korean. Let's practice this super useful pattern!

CRACKING THE PATTERN CODE

You attach **이에요** or **예요** to the noun without a space, based on the final letter of the noun. Use **이에요** if the noun ends with a consonant (받침) and **예요** if the noun ends with a vowel (no 받침).

N (받침 ○)	**이에요**	미국 사람 + 이에요 → 미국 사람이에요
N (받침 ×)	**예요**	친구 + 예요 → 친구예요

Be mindful of the linking sound when pronouncing final consonants (받침) with **-이에요**. For instance, in **미국 사람이에요**, the final consonant **ㅁ** in **사람** links to **-이에요**, creating the sound [**사라미에요**].

The basic form of N이에요/예요 is N이다 (to be N).

Tip!

In formal situations, **N입니다** is used regardless of whether the noun ends in a consonant or a vowel. For questions, use **N입니까?** to ask politely. You might hear this later, so take note!

반가워요 Nice to meet you. • 미국 사람 American (person) • 친구 friend

CORE SENTENCES

MP3 30

크리스	저는	크리스	예요.	I am Chris.
미국 사람	크리스 씨는	미국 사람	이에요.	Chris is an American.
학생	우리는	학생	이에요.	We are students.
영국 사람		영국 사람	이에요?	Are (you) British?
뭐		뭐	예요?	What is it?
누구		누구	예요?	Who is it?

Tip!

When talking about nationality, add the word **사람** (person) to the name of a country.

ex. **미국** (America) + **사람** (person) → **미국 사람** (American)

영국 (UK) + **사람** (person) → **영국 사람** (British)

EXPLORE FURTHER

Honorific Form of N이에요/예요: N이세요/세요

We sometimes say things a little differently to sound more polite, especially in public places. You'll often hear **N이세요/세요**, the honorific forms of **N이에요/예요**, in places like restaurants or stores. But when talking about yourself, just reply with **N이에요/예요**.

At a restaurant Staff: 몇 분**이세요**? How many people are in your group?

You: 두 명**이에요**. Two.

At the door A: 누구**세요**? Who are you?

B: 저**예요**! 제니**예요**. It's me. Jennie.

To ask about someone's name, age, or job, use **어떻게 되세요?** instead of **뭐예요?** to sound more polite. To answer, say **N이에요/예요**.

What is your name? → 이름이 뭐예요? *(casual)* / 이름이 어떻게 되세요? *(polite)*

What is your job? → 직업이 뭐예요? *(casual)* / 직업이 어떻게 되세요? *(polite)*

How old are you? → 몇 살이에요? *(casual)* / 나이가 어떻게 되세요? *(polite)*

Essential Practices

MP3 31

1. Circle the correct one and read it out loud.

(1) **김지수**이에요 / 예요. ~ am/is Kim Jisu.

(2) **영국 사람**이에요 / 예요. ~ am/is/are British.

(3) **점심시간**이에요 / 예요. It is lunch time.

(4) **학생**이에요 / 예요? Am/Are/Is ~ a student?

(5) 이름이 **뭐**이에요 / 예요? What is your name?

2. Use the given word in the N이에요/예요 pattern and say it out loud.

(1) 호주 사람 Australian → 호주 사람이에요. ~ am/are/is Australian.

(2) 요리사 cook/chef → ______. ~ am/are/is a cook.

(3) 회사원 office worker → ______. ~ am/are/is an office worker.

(4) 얼마 how much (the price) → ______? How much is it?

3. Use the hint words to complete the conversation. Then, practice reading it aloud.

(1) **뭐** A: 이름이 뭐예요? What is your name?
카일 B: 저는 카일이에요. I am Kyle.

(2) **한국 사람** A: ______? Are you Korean?
일본 사람 B: 아니요, ______. No, I am Japanese.

(3) **얼마** A: 이거 ______? How much is this?
만 원 B: ______. It's ₩10,000.

4. Now you can use N이에요/예요 to create a short self-introduction! Look at the example, write your own introduction.

ex. 안녕하세요! 저는 크리스예요 [Name]. 미국 사람이에요 [Nationality]. 선생님이에요 [Job]. 반갑습니다.

Hello! I am Chris. I am American. I am a teacher. Nice to meet you.

"안녕하세요? 저는 ______ [Name]. ______ [Nationality]. ______ [Job]. 반갑습니다."

UNIT 6

Question Words
질문 단어

Video 12

When speaking a foreign language, understanding questions is often harder than talking about yourself. Even if you are ready to answer, it won't help if you don't understand the question! While learning **N이에요/예요**, you've already learned how to ask basic questions like **뭐예요?** (What is it?), **누구예요?** (Who is it?), and **어디예요?** (Where is it?). Let's go one step further with other essential question words.

1 5Wh1H Question Words: 뭐, 누구, 어디, 언제, 왜, 어떻게

First, let's look at the 5Wh1H question words.

뭐	누구	어디	언제	왜	어떻게 [어떠케]
what	who	where	when	why	how

For nouns like **뭐**, **누구**, 어디, and **언제**, you add **-이에요/예요** to make questions. For adverbs like **왜** and **어떻게**, you simply add **-요?**. Try completing the question sentences below.

(1) **뭐**______? What is it?
(2) **누구**______? Who is it?
(3) **어디**______? Where is it?
(4) **언제**______? When is it?
(5) **왜**______? Why?
(6) **어떻게**______? How?

If you got this right, the sentences are **뭐예요?**, **누구예요?**, **어디예요?**, **언제예요?**, **왜요?**, and **어떻게요?**.

And here are three important things to remember when making questions:

① When **뭐** is used as an object, **뭐를** can be shortened to **뭘**. In casual speech, the object marker **을/를** is often left out.

뭐를 좋아해요? → **뭘** 좋아해요? / **뭐** 좋아해요? What do you like?

Tip!

뭐 appears as **무엇** in written Korean.

② 누구 changes to 누가 when used as a subject.

누구가 책을 읽어요? (✕) 누가 책을 읽어요? (○) Who reads the book?

③ When asking questions with adverbs like **왜**, **어떻게**, and sometimes **언제**, you can place the adverb either at the beginning of the sentence or right before the verb.

왜 한국어를 배워요? / 한국어를 **왜** 배워요? Why do you learn Korean?

언제 밥을 먹어요? / 밥을 **언제** 먹어요? When do you eat a meal?

☑ Self-Check

1. Match the question words to their English meanings.

누구	어디	뭐	어떻게	왜	언제
how	why	where	who	what	when

2. Complete the sentences using the correct question words. Use each word only once.

누구   누가   왜   어디   언제   뭐   뭘   어떻게

(1) Who is Mr. Mark? → ______ 마크 씨예요?

(2) Who is this person? → 이 사람은 ______예요?

(3) What is your name? → 이름이 ______예요?

(4) Why do you learn Korean? → ______ 한국어를 배워요?

(5) How do you go to Korea? → 한국에 ______ 가요?

(6) When is your birthday? → 생일이 ______예요?

(7) What are you eating? → ______ 먹어요?

(8) Where is that place? → 거기가 ______예요?

[Answer Key] **1.** 누구 - who 어디 - where 뭐 - what 어떻게 - how 왜 - why 언제 - when
2. (1) 누가 (2) 누구 (3) 뭐 (4) 왜 (5) 어떻게 (6) 언제 (7) 뭘 (8) 어디

2 Counting Question Word: 몇

When asking about numbers or amounts, use 몇, which means "how many." It is used with counters like 명 (for people), 시 (o'clock), 개 (for things), and many more.

몇 명 [면명] how many people　　몇 시 what time　　몇 개 how many things

Tip!
When counting people, you can also say 몇 사람 or 몇 분 (honorifics).

When you ask about the price, use 얼마 instead of 몇.

이거 몇이에요? (×)　　이거 몇 원이에요? (×)　　이거 얼마예요? (○) How much is this?

For questions with 몇 + counter, the answer will be a number with a counter. In the next unit, we'll learn how to read Korean numbers to answer these questions.

☑ Self-Check

1. Choose the correct counter.

명　　시　　개

(1) There are three apples. → 사과가 3_____ 있어요.

(2) I have five friends. → 친구가 5_____ 있어요.

(3) It's 4 o'clock → 지금은 4_____예요.

2. Complete the sentence by using 얼마 or 몇 + counter.

(1) __몇 명__이에요? How many people are you?
[면명]

(2) _________예요? What time is it?

(3) 사과가 _________ 있어요? How many apples do you have?

(4) 이거 _________예요? 비싸요? How much is this? Is it expensive?

(5) 가족이 _________ 있어요? How many family members do you have?

(6) 저 가방 _________예요? How much is that bag?

[Answer Key] **1.** (1) 개 (2) 명 (3) 시
2. (1) 몇 명 (2) 몇 시 (3) 몇 개 (4) 얼마 (5) 몇 명 (6) 얼마

3 Specific Question Words: 어느, 무슨, 어떤

Some question words are used to ask about specific choices or characteristics. In daily life, you will mostly use these three:

어느	무슨	어떤
which (among ~)	what kind of (category)	which (features)

You use these question words right before a noun. Their usages are slightly different.

어느 + N which (among known or limited options)	Used when choosing among specific, known, or limited options. A **어느 색**이 좋아요? 빨강? 노랑? Which color do you like? Red? Yellow? B 노랑이 좋아요. I like yellow.
무슨 + N what kind of (category, not person)	Used to ask about a type or category without specific options. Not used for people. A **무슨 노래**를 좋아해요? What kind of songs do you like? B 힙합을 좋아해요. I like hip-hop.
어떤 + N what kind of / which (with features)	Used to ask about the characteristics or nature of something or someone. A 알렉스 씨는 **어떤 사람**이에요? What kind of person is Alex? B 친절한 사람이에요. 그리고 똑똑해요. He is a kind person. And he is smart.

Although their uses differ slightly, you don't need to worry about making a perfect distinction. The self-check below is just a quick review, so don't worry too much. Native speakers often don't strictly separate them either!

☑ Self-Check

1. Fill in the blanks with 어느, 무슨, or 어떤 to complete each sentence.

(1) A ___무슨___ 노래 좋아해요? What kind of songs do you like?

B 케이팝을 좋아해요. I like K-pop.

(2) A 알렉스 씨는 __________ 사람이에요? What kind of person is Alex?

B 정말 착해요. 그리고 똑똑해요. He's very kind. And he's smart.

(3) A __________ 나라에 가요? 중국? 일본? Which country are you going to? China? Japan?

B 일본에 가요. I'm going to Japan.

[Answer Key] 1. (1) 무슨 (2) 어떤 (3) 어느

UNIT 7

Numbers

숫자

Video 13

In Korean, there are two types of numbers: **Sino-Korean numbers** and **native Korean numbers**. Each type is used in different situations. We'll look at the most common uses of each type and learn how to read them step by step. Practice by tracing the gray Korean letters and get used to the words.

1 Sino-Korean Numbers: 일, 이, 삼, 사, ...

Sino-Korean numbers are used when we talk about numbers themselves—like phone numbers, prices, dates, and so on. Let's start with the basic numbers from 0. Trace over the gray letters to practice writing the numbers.

0	1	2	3	4	5	6	7	8	9	10
영/공	일	이	삼	사	오	육	칠	팔	구	십
11	...	20	30	40	50	60	70	80	90	100
십일	...	이십	삼십	사십	오십	육십	칠십	팔십	구십	백

Tip!

People use **영** when reading **0** on its own, and use **공** when giving numbers like phone numbers.

Once you know the basic Sino-Korean numbers (일, 이, 삼...), it's easy to build bigger numbers. Think of them like building blocks—just combine them in a regular pattern.

To say numbers from 11 to 19, say 십 (10) first, then the number:

11 → 십일　　12 → 십이　　13 → 십삼　　...

For 20, 30, 40, and so on, say the number first, then 십:

20 → 이십　30 → 삼십　40 → 사십　…

The same rule applies to hundreds (백) and beyond:

100 → 백　200 → 이백　300 → 삼백　…

If you remember the pattern above, you can read three-digit numbers too! Try 23 → **이십삼**. What about 400? That's **사백**. And 333? That's **삼백삼십삼**.

The number 육 (6) is pronounced [뉵] when it follows a final consonant.

16 → 십육 [심뉵]　26 → 이십육 [이심뉵]　106 → 백육 [뱅뉵]

Now let's look at some larger numbers.

1,000	10,000	100,000	1,000,000	10,000,000
천	만	십만 [심만]	백만 [뱅만]	천만

When large numbers begin with 1, you don't say 일 (1).

10　**십** (일십 ×)

110　**백십** (일백일십 ×)

1,110　**천백십** (일천일백일십 ×)

…

As you can see from **만**, **십만**, **백만**, and **천만**, large numbers in Korean are based on units of **만** (ten thousand), not thousand like in English. This is especially important when talking about prices. When you read numbers in Korean, Imagine a break every 4 digits instead of every 3.

12,340 → 1|2,340 (만)　**만** 이천삼백사십

6,543,210 → 654|3,210 (만)　육백오십사**만** 삼천이백십

Tip!

The next large named units after **만** (10,000) are **억** (100 million) and **조** (1 trillion). These large units are often used in the news, when talking about prices, budgets, or population numbers.

☑ Self-Check

1. Write each number using Sino-Korean numbers.

(1) 11: 십일 (2) 25: ______

(3) 104: ______ (4) 6,400: ______

(5) 17,345: ______ (6) 357,896: ______

2. Look at the Sino-Korean numbers written in Korean and write them in digits.

(1) 오십이: 52 (2) 백삼: ______

(3) 천이백: ______ (4) 천오백십오: ______

(5) 만 이천삼백사십: ______ (6) 이십삼만 오천이백십삼: ______

3. Read and Say: How do you read the underlined number? Write the number in 한글, and then read it out loud.

(1) A 아메리카노 얼마예요? How much is an Americano?

B 4,500원 이에요. It's 4,500 won.
(원)

(2) A 화장실 비밀번호가 뭐예요? What's the bathroom passcode?

B 4 0 9 8 이에요. It's 4098.
( )

(3) A 방이 몇 층이에요? What floor is your room on?

B 6층 이에요. It's on the 6th floor.
(층)

(4) A 몇 번 버스를 타요? Which bus number do you take?

B 701번 버스를 타요. I take bus number 701.
(번)

[Answer Key]
1. (1) 십일 (2) 이십오 (3) 백사 (4) 육천사백 (5) 만 칠천삼백사십오 (6) 삼십오만 칠천팔백구십육
2. (1) 52 (2) 103 (3) 1,200 (4) 1,515 (5) 12,340 (6) 235,213
3. (1) 사천오백 (2) 사공구팔 / 사영구팔 (3) 육 (4) 칠백일 / 칠공일 / 칠영일

2 Native Korean Numbers: 하나, 둘, 셋, 넷, ...

Native Korean numbers are mostly used to count things like people, hours, items, and so on. You'll often see them with counters—special words that come after the number to show what you're counting, such as **명**, **사람**, or **개**.

Let's take a look at how to read numbers in native Korean.

1	2	3	4	5	6	7	8	9	10
하나 /한	둘 /두	셋 /세	넷 /네	다섯	여섯	일곱	여덟 [여덜]	아홉	열
11	**...**	**20**	**30**	**40**	**50**	**60**	**70**	**80**	**90**
열하나	...	스물 /스무	서른	마흔	쉰	예순	일흔	여든	아흔

You may have noticed that some numbers above have two forms. **하나**, **둘**, **셋**, **넷**, and **스물** are used on their own, but when combined with counters, they change to **한**, **두**, **세**, **네**, and **스무**. These changes make pronunciation smoother.

★ × 1

한 개 (not 하나 개)

★ × 2

두 개 (not 둘 개)

★ × 3

세 개 (not 셋 개)

★ × 4

네 개 (not 넷 개)

★ × 20

스무 개 (not 스물 개)

★ × 22

스물두 개 (not 스무둘 개)

Just like with Sino-Korean numbers, you can build larger numbers by combining smaller ones. 11 is **열** (10) + **하나** (1) → **열하나**, 22 is **스물** (20) + **셋** (3) → **스물셋**, and so on. What about 99? Yes, that's **아흔아홉**.

Native Korean numbers are usually used up to 99. For **백** (100) and above, people use Sino-Korean numbers instead. And Koreans often switch to Sino-Korean numbers for things over 20 in daily life, so you don't need to worry too much about using native numbers every time.

The counter you use depends on what you're counting. Take a look at the table on the next page. The yellow boxes show the things being counted, and the gray text below shows the counters you need. For example, when counting people, you use **명** or **사람**: **한 사람**, **두 사람**, **세 사람**... If you are counting people in an honorific way, such as people older or not close to you, you use **분** instead: **한 분**, **두 분**, **세 분**... The counters in the table are commonly used in daily life, so pay close attention to them.

사람 person	사람 Person (honorific)	물건 object	동물 animal	나이 age
명 / 사람	분	개	마리	살
시간 time (o'clock)	**시간** time (hours)	**컵** cup/glass	**병** bottle	**책** book
시	시간	잔	병	권

Tip!

You can add 들 after a noun to make it plural, like **사람** (person) → **사람들** (people). But in most cases, especially when you use numbers and counters, you don't need to say 들. Korean is not as strict as English about marking singular or plural.

☑ Self-Check

1. Read the digit and write it as native Korean number.

(1) 4: ___넷___ (2) 8: ________

(3) 10: ________ (4) 35: ________

(5) 21: ________ (6) 57: ________

2. Read the Korean number and write it in digits.

(1) 둘: ___2___ (2) 여섯: ________

(3) 아홉: ________ (4) 열여덟: ________

(5) 스물하나: ________ (6) 마흔셋: ________

3. Fill in the blank using a native Korean number + counter.

(1) There are four people. → 사람이 ___네 명___ 있어요.

(2) There are seven apples. → 사과가 ________ 있어요.

(3) I have two dogs. → 개가 ________ 있어요.

(4) It's 1 o'clock now. → 지금은 ________예요.

(5) I have thirteen books. → 책이 ________ 있어요.

(6) I am 24 years old. → 저는 ________이에요.

[Answer Key]
1. (1) 넷 (2) 여덟 (3) 열 (4) 서른다섯 (5) 스물하나 (6) 쉰일곱
2. (1) 2 (2) 6 (3) 9 (4) 18 (5) 21 (6) 43
3. (1) 네 명 (2) 일곱 개 (3) 두 마리 (4) 한 시 (5) 열세 권 (6) 스물네 살

UNIT 8

Time and Dates

시간과 날짜

Video 14

Now that you've learned numbers, it's time to use them to talk naturally about dates and time. With just a few key units and pronunciation tips, you'll be able to say the time and dates easily.

1 Time: 시 (o'clock), 분 (minute)

For the question **몇 시예요?** (What time is it?), the answer usually includes both the hour and minute. Place a native number before 시 (o'clock) and a Sino-Korean number before 분 (minute).

Native Korean Numbers		Sino-Korean Numbers	
한, 두, 세, 네, ...	**시** o'clock	**일, 이, 삼, 사, ...**	**분** minute

To read the time, just follow the order: native number + 시, Sino-Korean number + 분. You can also use 반 to mean "half past." Try reading the times below.

10 : 10	11 : 11	12 : 30
_____시 _____분	_____시 _____분	_____시 _____분 or _____시 반

If you read them correctly, they would sound like: 10:10 → 열 시 십 분, 11:11 → 열한 시 십일 분, and 12:30 → 열두 시 삼십 분 or 열두 시 반.

Tip!

"Second" in Korean is **초**, and it also uses Sino-Korean numbers: 30 seconds → **삼십 초**

There are also words that help describe the time of day more clearly:

a.m. before noon	p.m. afternoon	early morning (dawn)	morning	daytime (around noon)	evening	night
오전	오후	새벽	아침	낮	저녁	밤

In English, time words like a.m. or p.m. come after the hours. But in Korean, these words come before the hour.

2 a.m. → 오전 두 시   2 p.m. → 오후 두 시   2 in the morning → 새벽 두 시 …

Tip!

To say "at" a certain time, use the time marker **에**. For example, you can say **몇 시에 일어나요**? (What time do you wake up?) and **아침 일곱 시에 일어나요**. (I wake up at 7 in the morning.)

☑ Self-Check

1. Write the full time in Korean using 시 and 분.

(1) 2:10 → 두 시 십 분   (2) 5:11 → ________

(3) 12:25 → ________   (4) 7:30 → ________

(5) 10:23 → ________   (6) 3:47 → ________

2. Read the Korean time expressions and write the numbers.

(1) 여섯 시 십오 분 → 6 : 15   (2) 아홉 시 반 → ____ : ____

(3) 한 시 삼십 분 → ____ : ____   (4) 열한 시 이십 분 → ____ : ____

(5) 네 시 오 분 → ____ : ____   (6) 여덟 시 십칠 분 → ____ : ____

3. Write the full time in Korean using the correct word for time of day (오전, 오후, 아침, 낮, 저녁, 밤, 새벽).

(1) 2 in the morning : 새벽 두 시   (2) 3 p.m. : ________

(3) 12 daytime : ________   (4) 6 in the evening : ________

(5) 11 at night : ________   (6) 6:30 in the morning : ________

(7) 9 a.m. : ________   (8) 8 in the morning : ________

[Answer Key]
1. (1) 두 시 십 분 (2) 다섯 시 십일 분 (3) 열두 시 이십오 분 (4) 일곱 시 삼십 분 / 일곱 시 반 (5) 열 시 이십삼 분 (6) 세 시 사십칠 분
2. (1) 6:15 (2) 9:30 (3) 1:30 (4) 11:20 (5) 4:05 (6) 8:17
3. (1) 새벽 두 시 (2) 오후 세 시 (3) 낮 열두 시 (4) 저녁 여섯 시 (5) 밤 열한 시 (6) 아침 여섯 시 반 / 아침 여섯 시 삼십 분 (7) 오전 아홉 시 (8) 아침 여덟 시

2 Dates: 년 (year), 월 (month), 일 (day), 요일 (day of the week)

In Korean, dates are said in the order of 년 (year) → 월 (month) → 일 (day), from larger to smaller units. All parts use Sino-Korean numbers. Let's start with the biggest unit and work our way down.

1 Year: 몇 년이에요? (What year is it?)

You can ask the year by saying **몇 년이에요?** (몇 년 [면년]). Unlike in English, you don't split the year into two-digit parts. Read the year as one full number from the thousands, then add 년 (year).

1990년 → 천구백구십 년 (not "nineteen ninety")

2025년 → 이천이십오 년 (not "twenty twenty-five")

2 Month: 몇 월이에요? (What month is it?)

You ask the month by saying **몇 월이에요?** (몇 월 [며뒬]). Just add a Sino-Korean number before **월** (month). Watch out for two exceptions: 6월 → **유월** (not 육월), 10월 → **시월** (not 십월).

1월 January	2월 February	3월 March	4월 April	5월 May	6월 June
일월	이월	삼월	사월	오월	유월
7월 July	8월 August	9월 September	10월 October	11월 November	12월 December
칠월	팔월	구월	시월	십일월	십이월

3 Date: 며칠이에요? (What is the date?)

1일	2일	3일	4일	5일	6일	7일	8일	9일	10일
일일	이일	삼일	사일	오일	육일	칠일	팔일	구일	십일
11일	12일	13일	14일	15일	16일	17일	18일	19일	20일
십일일	십이일	십삼일	십사일	십오일	십육일 [심뉴길]	십칠일	십팔일	십구일	이십일
21일	22일	23일	24일	25일	26일	27일	28일	29일	30일
이십일일	이십이일	이십삼일	이십사일	이십오일	이십육일 [이십뉴길]	이십칠일	이십팔일	이십구일	삼십일
31일									
삼십일일									

The word **며칠** is originally from **몇** + **일**, but has been used so frequently that it became one fixed word. When answering the question **며칠이에요?**, people usually say the month and day together: **삼월 십오일이에요.** (It's March 15.)

Each day is made by combining a Sino-Korean number with **일**. Be careful with the pronunciation of 6 (**육**) after a **받침**.

16일 → 십육일 [심뉴길]   26일 → 이십육일 [이심뉴길]

4 Day of the Week: 무슨 요일이에요? (What day of the week is it?)

The word for "day of the week" is **요일**. Each day name is made by adding **요일** to a word that comes from **한자** (Chinese characters). When marking calendars or counting days of the week, people often drop the **요일** and just say **월**, **화**, **수**, **목**, **금**, **토**, **일**.

Monday	Tuesday	Wednesday	Thursday	Friday	Saturday	Sunday
월요일	**화**요일	**수**요일	**목**요일	**금**요일	**토**요일	**일**요일
Weekday					Weekend	
평일					주말	

To wrap up, try reading the circled date on the calendar below. Think in larger-to-smaller order.

8

월	화	수	목	금	토	일
	1	2	3	4	5	6
7	8	9	10	11	12	13
14	15	16	17	18	19	20
21	22	23	24	25	26	27
28	29	30	31			

2027년 8월 24일 목요일

→ 이천이십칠 **년** 팔 **월** 이십사 **일** 목 **요일**

☑ Self-Check

1. Read each date in Korean.

(1) 2030년 6월 15일 → ____________________

(2) 12월 31일 → ____________________

(3) 2026년 3월 2일 → ____________________

(4) 10월 9일 → ____________________

2. Look at the Korean date and write it in English month, day, year.

(1) 이천이십칠년 칠월 오일 → ____________________

(2) 이천이십오년 시월 십일일 → ____________________

3. Fill in the blanks with the correct words in Korean.

(1) **A** 오늘이 며칠이에요?

B ____________________이에요. (July 24, 2028)

(2) **A** 오늘이 무슨 요일이에요?

B ____________________이에요. (Thursday)

(3) **A** 생일이 언제예요?

B ____________________이에요. (June 5th)

4. Answer yourself! Write your own answers to each question.

(1) 생일이 언제예요? → ____________________

(2) 오늘이 무슨 요일이에요? → ____________________

(3) 오늘이 며칠이에요? → ____________________

[Answer Key] **1.** (1) 이천삼십년 유월 십오일 (2) 십이월 삼십일일 (3) 이천이십육년 삼월 이일 (4) 시월 구일
2. (1) July 5, 2027 (2) October 11, 2025
3. (1) 2028년 7월 24일 / 이천이십팔년 칠월 이십사일 (2) 목요일 (3) 6월 5일 / 유월 오일

UNIT 9

Ready to Make A/V Patterns ①: -아/어 Ending

형용사/동사 패턴 만들기 준비 ① : -아/어 어미

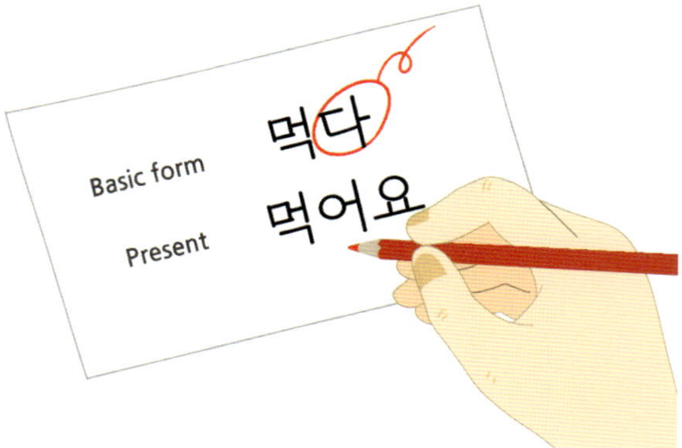

Video 15

So far, we've focused on essential words and noun-based patterns. Now let's move on to patterns that use verbs and adjectives. To do that, it's really helpful to understand two important endings: -아/어 and -(으). Many Korean grammar patterns begin with one of these endings. If you look at the table of contents of this book, you'll see these endings appear often. Let's start by learning how to attach the -아/어 ending.

1 Key Points of -아/어 Ending

When you change a verb or adjective to attach the -아/어 ending, look at the last vowel in the stem. That vowel tells you whether to use -아 or -어 (or sometimes -해).

보다 (stem: 보) | 만들다 (stem: 만들) | 맛있다 (stem: 맛있)

Here are the general rules.

1 If the final vowel of the stem is ㅏ or ㅗ → Add -아 to the stem.

ㅏ or ㅗ (○)
닫다 + -아
stem: 닫

2 If the final vowel is anything else → Add -어 to the stem.

ㅏ or ㅗ (×)
맛있다 + -어
stem: 맛있

3 If the verb or adjective ends in 하다 → Change 하 to 해.

말하다 + -해
stem

The pattern -아/어요 is one of the most common patterns that starts with -아/어. When you see this kind of pattern, think about whether to add -아요, -어요, or -해요, depending on the final vowel of the verb or adjective stem.

Let's take a look at how to turn each word into the -아/어요 form.

Word	Stem		Choose Ending		Stem + Ending		-아/어요 Form
닫다 to close	닫	+	-아	➡	닫아	➡	닫아요
맛있다 to be delicious	맛있	+	-어	➡	맛있어	➡	맛있어요
말하다 to say	말하	+	-해	➡	말해	➡	말해요

☑ Self-Check

1. Complete the table.

Word	Stem		Choose Ending		Stem + Ending		-아/어요 Form
좋다 to be good		+		→		→	
믿다 to believe		+		→		→	
필요하다 to need		+		→		→	

[Answer Key] 1. 좋다 → 좋 + 아 → 좋아 → 좋아요
믿다 → 믿 + 어 → 믿어 → 믿어요
필요하다 → 필요하 (drop 하) + 해 → 필요해 → 필요해요

2 The "Making It Short" Rule

If the stem ends in a vowel (with no 받침), the ending often becomes shorter to make pronunciation easier. These changes are called contractions. It's like writing the word the way it naturally sounds when spoken quickly.

1 If the stem already ends in ㅏ or ㅓ → Don't add -아 or -어 again.

already ends in ㅏ

가다 + -아 → 가아 → 가

stem

2 If the stem ends in ㅐ, ㅔ, or ㅕ, which already contains the shape of ㅓ → Don't add -어.

already has ㅓ

보내다 + -어 → 보내어 → 보내

stem

3 Combine the stem vowel and ending into a diphthong.

A diphthong is a sound where one vowel glides smoothly into the next—such as ㅘ, ㅝ, or ㅕ. The two vowels merge into a single syllable for smoother pronunciation.

merges ㅘ

보다 + -아 → 보아 → 봐

stem

Let's look at some examples of the -아/어요 pattern based on what we've just learned.

Word	Stem		Choose Ending		Stem + Ending		-아/어요 Form
가다 to go	가	+	-아	➡	가	➡	가요
서다 to stand	서	+	-어	➡	서	➡	서요
보내다 to send	보내	+	-어	➡	보내	➡	보내요
세다 to count	세	+	-어	➡	세	➡	세요
켜다 to turn on	켜	+	-어	➡	켜	➡	켜요

보다 to see/watch	보	+	-아	➡	봐	➡	봐요
배우다 to learn	배우	+	-어	➡	배워	➡	배워요
마시다 to drink	마시	+	-어	➡	마셔	➡	마셔요

☑ Self-Check

1. Complete the table for -아/어요.

Word	Stem		Choose Ending		Stem + Ending		-아/어요 Form
비싸다 to be expensive		+		➜		➜	
일어서다 to stand up		+		➜		➜	
지내다 to get along		+		➜		➜	
오다 to come		+		➜		➜	
알리다 to let someone know		+		➜		➜	

[Answer Key] 1. **비싸다** → 비싸 + ~~-아~~ → 비싸 → 비싸요 **일어서다** → 일어서 + ~~-어~~ → 일어서 → 일어서요 **지내다** → 지내 + ~~-어~~ → 지내 → 지내요 **오다** → 오 + -아 → 와 → 와요 **알리다** → 알리 + -어 → 알려 → 알려요

3 Wrap-up: Summary of -아/어 Rules

Let's review what you've learned:

- All in all, when attaching -아/어 to a stem, look at the final vowel in the stem to decide between -아 or -어.
- If the word ends in 하다, change 하 to 해.
- If the stem ends in a vowel (no 받침), contractions may apply.

☑ Self-Check

1. Complete the table for -아/어요.

Word	Stem	Choose Ending	Stem + Ending	-아/어요 Form
닫다		+	→	→
맛있다		+	→	→
말하다		+	→	→
가다		+	→	→
서다		+	→	→
보내다		+	→	→
세다		+	→	→
켜다		+	→	→
보다		+	→	→
배우다		+	→	→
마시다		+	→	→

[Answer Key] 1. **닫다** → 닫 + 아 → 닫아 → 닫아요 **맛있다** → 맛있 + 어 → 맛있어 → 맛있어요 **말하다** → 말~~하~~ + 해 → 말해 → 말해요
가다 → 가 + ~~아~~× → 가 → 가요 **서다** → 서 + ~~어~~× → 서 → 서요 **보내다** → 보내 + ~~어~~× → 보내 → 보내요
세다 → 세 + ~~어~~× → 세 → 세요 **켜다** → 켜 + ~~어~~× → 켜 → 켜요
보다 → 보 + 아 → 봐 → 봐요 **배우다** → 배우 + 어 → 배워 → 배워요 **마시다** → 마시 + 어 → 마셔 → 마셔요

UNIT 10 A/V-아/어요

Present Tense Adjective/Verb

Video 16

The pattern -아/어요 is your go-to tool for expressing the present tense in informal but polite speech. It's used in all four sentence types: statements, questions, commands, and suggestions. We already learned how to attach -아/어 in a previous unit. Now let's do a quick review and practice it with useful verbs and adjectives. You'll also come across a few irregular forms when we look at the core sentences.

CRACKING THE PATTERN CODE

Whether you attach -아요 or -어요 depends on the vowel in the final syllable of the verb or adjective stem. If the final vowel is ㅏ or ㅗ, add -아요. If it's anything else, add -어요. For words ending in 하다, change it to 해요.

ㅏ, ㅗ (O)	+ -아요	앉다 → 앉 + -아요 → 앉아요 [안자요] └ vowel ㅏ(O)
ㅏ, ㅗ (X)	+ -어요	먹다 → 먹 + -어요 → 먹어요 └ vowel ㅓ (not ㅏ, ㅗ)
-하다	→ -해요	일하다 → 일해요

When the stem ends in a vowel with no final consonant (받침), contractions often happen.

1 If the stem ends in ㅏ or ㅓ, don't add another -아 or -어.

가다 → ㄱㅏ + ~~아~~요 → 가요 (not 가아요)

서다 → ㅅㅓ + ~~어~~요 → 서요 (not 서어요)

2 If the stem ends in ㅐ, ㅔ, or ㅕ, which already contains the shape of ㅓ, don't add -어.

보내다 → 보ㄴㅐ + ~~어~~요 → 보내요 (not 보내어요)
└ ㅐ includes ㅓ shape in it

3 Combine the stem vowel and ending into a diphthong.

오다 → 오 + 아요 → 와요 (not 오아요)
↳ ㅗ + ㅏ = ㅘ

마시다 → 마ㅅㅣ + 어요 → 마셔요 (not 마시어요)
↳ ㅣ + ㅓ = ㅕ

Tip!

If you add just -아/어 or -해 without 요, it becomes 반말 (casual speech). For example, 가요 is informal polite, while 가 is casual.

CORE SENTENCES

MP3 32

좋다	좋아요!	It's good!
맛있다	맛있어요.	It's delicious!
좋아하다	한국 드라마를 좋아해요.	I like Korean dramas.
가다	어디 가요?	Where are you going?
보다	영화를 봐요.	I'm watching a movie.
마시다	우리 커피 마셔요!	Let's drink coffee!
쓰다*	일기를 써요.	I write in my journal.
바쁘다*	오늘은 바빠요.	I am busy today.
빠르다*	택시가 빨라요.	The taxi is fast.
배부르다*	배불러요.	I am full.

* irregular form (ㅡ disappears, 르 → ㄹㄹ)

Tip!

Irregular forms follow extra rules based on the final letter of the stem. For example, **쓰다** and **바쁘다** are "**ㅡ irregular**," while **부르다** and **배부르다** are "**르 irregular**." Check the Explore Further at the end of this unit.

뭐 what • 하다 to do • 일하다 to work • 앉다 [안따] to sit • 먹다 to eat • 가다 to go • 서다 to stand, to stop • 보내다 to send, to spend time • 오다 to come • 마시다 to drink

Essential Practices

MP3 33

1. Convert the given verb/adjective into the -아/어요 form and read it aloud.

좋다 → 좋아요 to be good	맛있다 → ______ to be delicious	좋아하다 → ______ to like
가다 → ______ to go	짜다 → ______ to be salty	보내다 → ______ to send
보다 → ______ to see/watch	배우다 → ______ to learn	쓰다* → ______ to write, to use
바쁘다* → ______ to be busy	배부르다* → ______ to be full	빠르다* → ______ to be fast

2. Use the hint words to complete the sentence with the correct -아/어요 form to match the English translation.

(1) 좋다 to be good — The weather is good. → 날씨가 좋아요.

(2) 먹다 to eat — Let's eat. → 우리 밥 ______.

(3) 오다 to come — When do you come? → 언제 ______?

(4) 배부르다* to be full — Are you full now? → 지금 ______?

(5) 빠르다* to be fast — The internet is fast here. → 여기 인터넷이 ______.

(6) 쓰다 to write — I'm writing a letter. → 편지를 ______.

(7) 바쁘다* to be busy — I'm too busy these days. → 요즘 너무 ______.

3. Complete the dialogues using the hint words, then read them aloud.

(1) **일하다** A: 지금 ______? Are you working now?
쓰다* B: 아니요, 일기 ______. No, I am writing a journal.

(2) **보다** A: 우리 영화 ______. Let's watch a movie.
바쁘다* B: 미안해요. 오늘은 ______. Sorry, I am busy today.

(3) **맛있다** A: 음식이 어때요? ______? How's the food? Is it delicious?
짜다 B: 음, 아니요. 너무 ______. Well, no. It's too salty.

(4) 배우다　A: 왜 한국어를 ________________? Why do you learn Korean?
좋아하다　B: 한국 드라마를 ________________. I like Korean dramas.

(5) 하다　A: 지금 뭐 ________________? What are you doing now?
읽다　B: 책 ________________. I'm reading a book.

(6) 마시다　A: 우리 커피 ________________. Let's drink coffee.
가다　B: 좋아요. 카페에 ________________. Sounds good. Let's go to a café.

EXPLORE FURTHER

ㅡ Irregular Rule & 르 Irregular Rule

In this unit, you saw two common irregular forms. Each is named after the final letter of the stem, because that letter changes when you conjugate the word. The ㅡ irregular rule always works. The 르 irregular rule also works nearly every time. Think of it as 99%! So when you add -아/어 to a stem ending in ㅡ or 르, just apply these rules.

1 ㅡ disappears before -아/어

If the stem ends in ㅡ, always drop the ㅡ before adding **-아** or **-어**. Check the vowel in the syllable before it to decide between **-아** or **-어**.

쓰다 → ㅆ + -어요 → **써요**
└ Use -어요 because there's no ㅏ or ㅗ before 쓰.

바쁘다 → 바ㅃ + -아요 → **바빠요**
└ Use -아요 because the vowel before 쁘 is ㅏ.

Try it yourself: **아프다** (to be sick, to hurt) → **아파요**, and **크다** (to be big) → **커요**.

2 르 → ㄹㄹ before -아/어

If the stem ends in 르, always change **르** to **ㄹㄹ** and then add **-아** or **-어**. Again, check the vowel just before **르** to decide which ending to use.

빠르다 → 빠ㄹㄹ + -아요 → **빨라요**
└ Use -아요 because the vowel before 르 is ㅏ.

배부르다 → 배부ㄹㄹ + -어요 → **배불러요**
└ Use -어요 because there's no ㅏ or ㅗ before 르.

Try it yourself: **모르다** (not to know) → **몰라요**, and **누르다** (to press) → **눌러요**.

UNIT **11**

안 A/V, 못 V

not A/V, cannot V

Video 17

Now that you've learned how to express general states or actions with **-아/어요**, let's explore negative forms. To make a negative sentence, simply place **안** (not) or **못** (can't) before the verb or adjective.

CRACKING THE PATTERN CODE

안 is used for simple negation or when you choose not to do something. It can be used with both verbs and adjectives. 못 means you can't do something because of ability or circumstances, and it's only used with verbs. Both 안 and 못 go right before the verb or adjective.

안 A/V not A, don't V	**안** 바빠요 not busy / **안** 해요 don't do
못 V can't V	**못** 해요 can't do

For **N + 하다** verbs, which are made by attaching -**하다** to an activity-related noun, place 안 or 못 between the noun and **하다**. In this case, the object marker **을/를** is usually attached to the noun.

공부**하다** ↔ 공부(를) **안** 해요 / 공부(를) **못** 해요
↳ 공부(N)+하다 — don't study / can't study

운동**하다** ↔ 운동(을) **안** 해요 / 운동(을) **못** 해요
↳ 운동(N)+하다 — don't exercise / can't exercise

Some verbs, like **좋아하다**, are not N+하다 combinations. Just negate them directly as 안 **좋아하다**.

Tip!

You might also hear -**지 않아요** ("not," like **안**) and -**지 못해요** ("cannot," like **못**). These forms sound a bit gentler and more polite. Just attach -**지 않아요** or -**지 못해요** to the verb or adjective stem.

• **Ready-Made Opposites:** Some verbs and adjectives have built-in opposites that naturally express negation, so 안 or 못 isn't used.

알아요 know	↔	몰라요 (안 알아요 ✕) don't know		
있어요 have / there is	↔	없어요 (안 있어요 ✕) don't have / there isn't		
맛있어요 delicious	↔	맛없어요 (안 맛있어요 ✕) not delicious		
재미있어요 fun	↔	재미없어요 (안 재미있어요 ✕) not fun		

For N이에요/예요 (am/are/is N), use N이/가 아니에요 for negation.

N이에요/예요 ↔ N이/가 아니에요 (안 N이에요 ✕)

CORE SENTENCES

MP3 34

	Q	A
춥다*	Q. 추워요? Is it cold?	A. 아니요, 안 추워요. No, it's not cold.
맵다*	Q. 김치가 매워요? Is kimchi spicy?	A. 아니요, 안 매워요. No, it's not spicy.
마시다	Q. 술 마셔요? Do you drink alcohol?	A. 술 안 마셔요. I don't drink alcohol. A. 술 못 마셔요. I can't drink alcohol.
수영하다	Q. 수영해요? Do you swim?	A. 저는 수영 안 해요. I don't/won't swim. A. 저는 수영 못 해요. I can't swim.
알다	Q. 이 사람 알아요? Do you know this person?	A. 아니요, 몰라요. No, I don't know.
맛있다	Q. 그 파스타 맛있어요? [마시써요] Is that pasta delicious?	A. 아니요, 맛없어요. [마덥써요] No, it's not delicious.
N이에요/예요	Q. 영국 사람이에요? Are you British?	A. 영국 사람이 아니에요. I am not British.

* irregular form (ㅂ → 우)

공부하다 to study • 운동하다 to exercise • 알다 to know • 모르다 not to know • 없다[업따] not to have, not to be • 맛있다[마시따] to be delicious • 맛없다[마덥따] to taste bad • 재미있다 to be fun • 재미없다[재미업따] not to be fun

Essential Practices

MP3 35

1. Fill in the table with the correct -아/어요 forms and negative forms.

Negating an Adjective (안)

Basic Form	-아/어요	Negative
좋다 to be good	좋아요	안 좋아요
짜다 to be salty		
바쁘다* to be busy		
빠르다* to be fast		
춥다* to be cold	추워요	
맵다* to be spicy		

Negating a Verb (안: don't / 못: can't)

Basic Form	-아/어요	don't	can't
먹다 to eat			
마시다 to drink			
쓰다* to write, to use			
수영하다 to swim		수영 안 해요	
운동하다 to exercise			

Ready-Made Opposites

Basic Form	-아/어요	Negative
알다 to know		
있다 to be, to have		
맛있다 to be delicious		
재미있다 to be fun		
영국 사람이다 to be British		
친구이다 to be a friend	친구예요	

2. Complete the sentences using the hint words and 안 or 못 to match the English translation.

(1) 마시다 to drink — I don't drink alcohol. = 저는 술을 ___안 마셔요___.

(2) 맵다* to be spicy — This kimchi isn't spicy. = 이 김치는 ________.

(3) 쓰다* to use — I don't use a smartphone. = 저는 스마트폰을 ________.

(4) 요리하다 to cook — I'm so busy. I don't cook. = 너무 바빠요. 그래서 ________.

(5) 먹다 to eat — I am too full. So I can't eat any more.
= 너무 배불러요. 그래서 더 ________.

3. **Complete the "no" response and say them aloud.**

(1) A: 오늘 **추워요**? Is it cold today?

B: 아니요, 안 추워요. No, it's not cold.

(2) A: 이 영화 **알아요**? Do you know this movie?

B: 아니요, ______________. No, I don't know.

(3) A: 우리 같이 **수영해요**! Let's swim together!

B: 아, 저는 수영을 ______________. Ah, I can't swim.

(4) A: 이거 **맛있어요**? Is this delicious?

B: 아니요, ______________. 너무 짜요. No, it's not delicious. It's too salty.

(5) A: 혹시 저 사람 마크 씨**예요**? Is that person Mark, by any chance?

B: 아니요, 마크 씨가 ______________. No, that's not Mark.

EXPLORE FURTHER

ㅂ Irregular Rule

Some verb stems and adjective stems that end in ㅂ follow the ㅂ **irregular** rule. When the stem ends in ㅂ and is followed by a vowel ending like **-아/어** or **-으**, the ㅂ **changes to 우** and combines with the ending.

ㅂ → 우 before -아/어, -으

맵다 → **매워요**

맵 + -어요 → 매우 + -어요 → **매워요**

↳ Use -어요 because there's no ㅏ or ㅗ before ㅂ.

돕다 → **도와요**

돕 + -아요 → 도우 + -아요 → **도와요**

↳ Use -아요 because the vowel before ㅂ is ㅗ.

When you say it quickly, **우 + 어** sounds like **워**, and **우 + 아** sounds like **와**. That's why **매우 + 어요** becomes **매워요**, and **도우 + 아요** becomes **도와요**.

You'll see the ㅂ irregular form in many everyday words.

춥다 (to be cold)	→	**추워요**	**덥다** (to be hot)	→	**더워요**
쉽다 (to be easy)	→	**쉬워요**	**어렵다** (to be difficult)	→	**어려워요**

Not all ㅂ-ending verbs are irregular. Some keep the ㅂ and follow the regular rules, like **입다** (to wear) → **입어요** and **잡다** (to hold) → **잡아요**.

Unlike the ㅡ and 르 irregular rules, which only apply before **-아/어** endings, the ㅂ irregular rule applies before both **-아/어** and **-으** endings. You'll learn more about **-(으)** patterns soon, so you'll see this rule again later!

UNIT **12**

V-아/어 주세요

Please V (for me)

Video 18

In public places, you'll often need to ask someone to do something for you, or respond to requests from others. That's where the **-아/어 주세요** pattern is useful. It lets you politely request someone to do something for you. Since this pattern is used to ask for actions, it only applies to verbs, not adjectives.

CRACKING THE PATTERN CODE

The pattern -아/어 주세요 follows the same rules as -아/어요 because they share the same base structure.

ㅏ, ㅗ (O)	+ **-아 주세요**	닫다 → 닫 + -아 주세요 → 닫아 주세요 (└ vowel ㅏ(O))
ㅏ, ㅗ (X)	+ **-어 주세요**	열다 → 열 + -어 주세요 → 열어 주세요 (└ vowel ㅓ (not ㅏ, ㅗ))
-하다	→ **-해 주세요**	말하다 → 말해 주세요

Contraction rules also apply.

사다 → ㅅㅏ + ~~아~~ 주세요 → **사 주세요** (not 사아 주세요)

세다 → ㅅㅔ + ~~어~~ 주세요 → **세 주세요** (not 세어 주세요)

보이다 → 보ㅇㅣ + 어 주세요 → **보여 주세요** (not 보이어 주세요)

여권 [여꿘] passport • 보이다 to show • 닫다 to close • 열다 to open • 말하다 to say, to speak • 사다 to buy • 세다 to count • 주다 to give

When requesting an object rather than an action, use N(을/를) 주세요 to ask for it. In everyday conversations, the object marker 을/를 is often omitted. N 주세요 means "I'd like N" when ordering food.

N 주세요 Please give N (to me)

To make a request softer or less demanding, you can add the adverb 좀 (a little) before -아/어 주세요 (e.g., 좀 열어 주세요) or between a noun and 주세요 (e.g., 물 좀 주세요).

CORE SENTENCES

MP3 36

N 주세요

		비빔밥 하나	주세요. One bibimbap, please.
		메뉴	좀 주세요. Please give me the menu.

V-아/어 주세요

가다	인천 공항으로	가	주세요. Please go to Incheon International Airport.
말하다	다시	말해	주세요. Tell me again, please.
기다리다	잠시만	기다려	주세요. Please wait for just a moment.
바꾸다	이것 좀	바꿔	주세요. Please change this.
쓰다*	여기에 이름을	써	주세요. Please write your name here.
돕다*	저 좀	도와	주세요. Please help me.

* irregular form (ㅡ disappears, ㅂ → 우)

Tip!

도와주세요 is so common it's written as one word without a space.

Essential Practices

MP3 37

1. Change each verb into the -아/어 주세요 form.

닫다 → ______ to close	열다 → ______ to open	가다 → ______ to go
알리다 → ______ to let someone know	기다리다 → ______ to wait	바꾸다 → ______ to change
확인하다 → ______ to check	돕다* → ______ to help	쓰다* → ______ to write, to use

2. Complete the sentences using the hint words and -아/어 주세요 to match the English translation.

(1) 말하다 to speak — Excuse me, but please speak a little slowly.
→ 죄송하지만 조금 천천히 말해 주세요.

(2) 돕다* to help — Excuse me, please help me.
→ 죄송한데 저 좀 ______.

(3) 열다 to open — Excuse me, please open the door.
→ 죄송하지만 문 좀 ______.

(4) 닫다 to close — It's too cold. Please close the window.
→ 너무 추워요. 창문 좀 ______.

(5) 가다 to go — (In a taxi) Please go to Seoul Station.
→ 서울역으로 ______.

(6) 확인하다 to check — (At a hotel) Please check the checkout time.
→ 체크아웃 시간을 ______.

(7) 바꾸다 to change — (At a hotel) The room is a bit dirty. Please give me another one.
→ 방이 좀 더러워요. 방을 ______.

(8) 물 water — Excuse me, please give me some water.
→ 죄송한데 여기 ______ 좀 ______.

Tip!

Starting your sentence with phrases like **죄송하지만** or **죄송한데**, which mean "Excuse me, but...," can make your request sound even more polite.

3. **Complete the dialogues using the hint words, then read them aloud.**

(1) 말하다
A: 이름을 ________________. Please tell me your name.
B: 제 이름은 존 스미스예요. My name is John Smith.

(2) 보다
A: 여러분! 여기 좀 ________________. Everyone, please look here!
B: 네! Sure!

(3) 보내다 / 알리다
A: 방학에 편지 ________________. Please send me a letter during school vacation.
B: 좋아요. 주소 ________________. Okay. Please tell me your address.

(4) 김치찌개 / 기다리다
A: 주문하시겠어요? May I take your order?
B: ________________ 하나 주세요. One kimchi jjigae, please.
A: 네, 잠시만 ________________________________. Okay, please wait for a moment.

EXPLORE FURTHER

"물은 셀프입니다"? What does it mean?

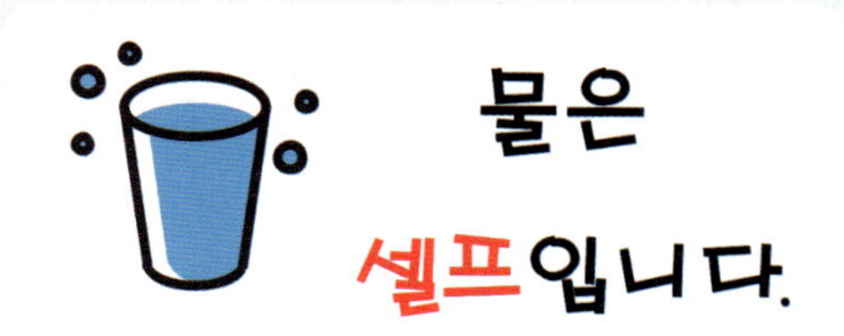

At many casual restaurants in Korea, water is usually free. It may be served at your table without you even asking—so don't be surprised! If you want more, just say **물 좀 더 주세요** (Please give me more water). Also, Korean meals often come with free side dishes like kimchi or pickles, called **반찬**. You can ask for more by saying **반찬 좀 더 주세요** (Please give me more side dishes).

Sometimes, you might see a sign that says **물은 셀프입니다**. What does that mean? "Water is self-serve." In other words, you have to get your own water from a water station. If you can't see it, you can simply ask: **물이 어디에 있어요**? (Where is the water?), using the **N이/가 있어요** pattern you learned earlier.

UNIT 13

V-아/어도 돼요?

Is it okay if I ~? (May/Can I ~?)

Video 19

When you're in a new place or culture, you might wonder: "Is it okay to do this?" or "Can I do that?" This is where the pattern **-아/어도 돼요?** comes in. This pattern is used to politely ask for permission or check if something is allowed or available. For example, you can use this pattern to ask if it's okay to sit somewhere, take photos, or pay with a card. It helps you navigate unfamiliar situations with confidence and respect.

CRACKING THE PATTERN CODE

The pattern -아/어도 돼요? follows the same conjugation rules as -아/어요. All you need to do is determine whether to attach -아, -어, or -해 based on the final vowel of the verb stem. If the stem ends in a vowel, remember that contraction rules apply.

ㅏ, ㅗ (○) +	**-아도 돼요**	들어가다 → 들어가 + **-아도 돼요** → **들어가도 돼요** (└→ vowel ㅏ(○))
ㅏ, ㅗ (×) +	**-어도 돼요**	먹다 → 먹 + **-어도 돼요** → **먹어도 돼요** (└→ vowel ㅓ (not ㅏ, ㅗ))
-하다 →	**-해도 돼요**	전화하다 → **전화해도 돼요**

The verb **돼요** comes from **되다** (to become, to be allowed). **되** + **어요** becomes **돼요**. You can also use **N 돼요?** to ask if something is available or accepted—not just with actions.

N 돼요? Is N available/accepted?

카드 돼요? Do you accept credit cards?

와이파이 돼요? Is Wi-Fi available?

테이크아웃 돼요? Is takeout available?

들어가다 to enter • 전화하다 to make a phone call • 카드 credit/debit card • 와이파이 Wi-Fi • 테이크아웃 takeout • 괜찮다[괜찬타] to be fine/okay

You can also use **V-아/어도 괜찮아요?** with the same meaning as **V-아/어도 돼요?**. However, **N 괜찮아요?** (Is N okay with you?) is not used in this context.

V-아/어도 돼요? Is it okay if I ~?	=	V-아/어도 괜찮아요? [괜차나요]	Is it okay if I ~?
N 돼요? Is N available/accepted?	≠	N 괜찮아요 ? [괜차나요]	Is N okay with you?

As a response to **V-아/어도 돼요?** or **N 돼요?**, you'll hear answers such as **네, 돼요/됩니다** or **아니요, 안 돼요/안 됩니다**. You can also simply repeat the phrase with a falling intonation, ending it with a period instead of a question mark.

Tip!

You might also use **되나요?** or **될까요?**. They mean the same as **돼요?**, but sound a bit more polite or gentle.

CORE SENTENCES

MP3 38

N 돼요?

여기 **와이파이** 돼요? Is Wi-Fi available here?

죄송한데 **포장** 돼요? Excuse me, can I get this to go?

V-아/어도 돼요?

앉다	여기 **앉아** 도 돼요?	Can I sit here?
사진 찍다	**사진 찍어** 도 돼요?	Is it okay to take a photo?
보다	잠깐 **봐** 도 돼요?	May I take a look for a moment?
입어 보다	**입어 봐** 도 돼요?	Can I try this (outfit) on?
마시다	이 물 **마셔** 도 돼요?	May I drink this water?
쓰다*	이 컵 **써** 도 돼요?	May I use this cup?

* irregular form (ㅡ disappears)

Tip!

The phrase **입어 보다** (to try on) combines **입다** + **-아/어 보다**. The **V-아/어 보다** pattern means "to try V-ing" or "to experience V-ing."

Essential Practices

MP3 39

1. Convert the given verbs into the -아/어도 돼요 form and read them aloud.

앉다 → 앉아도 돼요 to sit	사진 찍다 → ________ to take a photo	열다 → ________ to open
쓰다* → ________ to use, to write	운동하다 → ________ to exercise	전화하다 → ________ to make a phone call
들어가다 → ________ to enter	사다 → ________ to buy	켜다 → ________ to turn on
마시다 → ________ to drink	시키다 → ________ to order	보다 → ________ to see/watch
입어 보다 → 입어 봐도 돼요 to try on	열어 보다 → ________ to try opening	먹어 보다 → ________ to try eating

2. Complete the dialogues using the hint words and the -아/어도 돼요? or N 돼요? pattern.

~~쓰다* to use, to write~~	포장 take-out	열어 보다 to try opening
입어 보다 to try on	전화하다 to call (on the phone)	사진 찍다 to take a photo

(1) You want to know if you can use the Wi-Fi in a café.

A: 죄송한데 여기 와이파이 좀 써도 돼요 ? Excuse me, may I use the Wi-Fi here?

B: 네, 됩니다. Yes, you may.

A: 감사합니다! 비밀번호 좀 알려 주세요. Thank you! Please tell me the password.

(2) Your friend gave you a gift and you want to check if it's okay to open it now.

A: 생일 축하해요! 여기 선물이에요. Happy birthday! Here's a gift for you.

B: 와, 고마워요! 지금 ____________? Wow, thank you! Can I open it now?

(3) You want to ask if it's okay to call to your friend.

A: 이따 ____________? Is it okay if I call you later?

B: 그럼요. 전화해도 돼요. Of course. You can call me.

(4) After eating, you have leftovers and want to ask if you can take them out.

A: 죄송한데 이거 ______________________? Excuse me, can I take this to go?

B: 네, 됩니다. 잠시만 기다려 주세요. Yes, of course. Just a moment, please.

(5) You're at an art gallery and want to ask if you're allowed to take photos.

A: 혹시 ______________________? By any chance, may I take a photo?

B: 죄송합니다. 사진은 안 돼요. I am sorry. Photos are not allowed.

(6) At a clothing store, you've found a piece of clothing you like. You want to ask if you can try it on.

A: 이 옷 ______________________? May I try on these clothes?

B: 네, 그럼요. Yes, of course.

EXPLORE FURTHER

안 -아/어도 돼요 vs. -(으)면 안 돼요

When someone asks you **-아/어도 돼요?**, it's helpful to know how to respond—especially when something is not allowed.

If it's okay or allowed, say: **-아/어도 돼요**. (You can ~. / It's okay to ~.)

If it's not okay or not allowed, use a different pattern: **-(으)면 안 돼요**. (You shouldn't ~. / It's not allowed to ~.)

Note that **안 -아/어도 돼요** does NOT mean "not allowed." Instead, it means "don't have to do," indicating that the action is optional.

먹어도 돼요. You may eat.

먹으면 안 돼요. You shouldn't eat.

안 먹어도 돼요. You don't have to eat.

UNIT 14

A/V-았/었어요

Past Tense Adjective/Verb

Video 20

The pattern **-았/었어요** uses the past tense ending **-았/었-**, which shows that something already happened. You can think of it as the Korean way to say something happened in the past—like "I ate" or "It was good."

CRACKING THE PATTERN CODE

To form the past tense in Korean, simply attach -았어요, -었어요, or -했어요 to the stem, following the same principles as -아/어요.

ㅏ, ㅗ (O)	+ -았어요	좋다 → 좋 + -았어요 → 좋았어요 [조아써요] (└→ vowel ㅗ(O))
ㅏ, ㅗ (×)	+ -었어요	맛있다 → 맛있 + -었어요 → 맛있었어요 [마시써써요] (└→ vowel ㅣ (not ㅏ, ㅗ))
-하다	→ -했어요	말하다 → 말했어요 [말해써요]

Just like -아/어요, contractions occur when the stem ends in a vowel.

사다 → ㅅㅏ + -았어요 → 샀어요 (not 사았어요)

보내다 → 보ㄴㅐ + -았어요 → 보냈어요 (not 보내었어요)

오다 → 오 + -았어요 → 왔어요 (not 오았어요)

정말 really • 좋다[조타] to be good

For **N이에요/예요** (am/are/is N), the past tense is **N이었어요/였어요**. And **N이/가 아니에요** (am/are/is not N) becomes **N이/가 아니었어요** in the past tense.

N이에요/예요 ~ am/are/is N	→	N이었어요/였어요 ~ was/were N
N이/가 아니에요 ~ am/are/is not N	→	N이/가 아니었어요 ~ was/were not N

Tip!

The past tense ending -았/었- also appears in other patterns to add a past meaning. It's also used in formal speech (-**습니다** ending style): -았/었어요 → -았/었습니다, -했어요 → -했습니다.

CORE SENTENCES

MP3 40

먹다	밥	**먹었어요** ?	Did you eat a meal?
하다	어제 뭐	**했어요** ?	What did you do yesterday?
연습하다	한국어 말하기	**연습했어요** .	I practiced Korean speaking.
보내다	주말 잘	**보냈어요** ?	Did you have a good weekend?
감기(에) 걸리다		**감기(에) 걸렸어요** .	I caught a cold.
아프다 (아파요)*	어제 배가	**아팠어요** .	My stomach hurt yesterday.
부르다 (불러요)*	노래를	**불렀어요** .	I sang a song.
듣다 (들어요)*	음악을	**들었어요** .	I listened to music.

* irregular form (ㅡ disappears, ㄷ → ㄹ)

Essential Practices

MP3 41

1. For each word, write both the present and past forms.

	present	past		present	past
좋다 to be good →	좋아요	좋았어요	재미있다 to be fun →	______	______
연습하다 to practice →	______	______	피곤하다 to be tired →	______	______
자다 to sleep →	______	______	보내다 to send, to spend time →	______	______
주다 to give →	______	______	배우다 to learn →	______	______
부르다* to sing, to call someone →	______	______	빠르다* to be fast →	______	______
아프다* to be sick, to hurt →	______	______	쓰다* to write, to use →	______	______
듣다* to listen →	______	______	걷다* to walk →	걸어요	______

2. Complete the sentences using the hint word and the -았/었어요 pattern.

(1) 좋다 to be good
Was the weather good yesterday?
→ 어제 날씨 ____________________?

(2) 보내다 to spend time
Did you have a good weekend?
→ 주말 잘 ____________________?

(3) 연습하다 to practice
I practiced Korean pronunciation.
→ 한국어 발음을 ____________________.

(4) 쓰다* to write
I wrote a letter.
→ 편지를 ____________________.

(5) 아프다* to be sick
I had a headache yesterday.
→ 어제 머리가 ____________________.

(6) 걷다* to walk
I walked for a while.
→ 잠깐 ____________________.

3. **Complete the dialogues using the hint words. Then read them aloud.**

(1) 사다
주다
A: 이 꽃 ___샀어요___? Did you buy this flower?
B: 아니요, 친구가 ___줬어요___. No, my friend gave it to me.

(2) 하다
듣다*
A: 어제 저녁에 뭐 ________________? What did you do yesterday evening?
B: 음악 ________________. I listened to music.

(3) 재미있다
부르다*
A: 어제 노래방 ________________? Did you have fun at karaoke yesterday?
B: 네! 노래를 많이 ________________. Yes! I sang a lot of songs.

(4) 자다
피곤하다
A: 어제 일찍 ________________? Did you go to bed early yesterday?
B: 네, ________________. Yes, I was tired.

(5) 먹다
못 먹다
A: 밥 ________________? Did you have a meal?
B: 아니요, ________________. 바빴어요. No, I couldn't eat. I was busy.

(6) 감기 걸리다
가다
먹다
A: 저 ________________. I caught a cold.
B: 아이고, 병원 ________________? Oh no, did you go to the hospital?
A: 아니요, 그냥 약 ________________. No, I just took some medicine.

EXPLORE FURTHER

ㄷ Irregular Rule

Some verb stems that end in ㄷ change the ㄷ to ㄹ when followed by a vowel ending like **-아/어** or **-으**. This is called the **ㄷ irregular** rule. In this unit, you learned the verbs **듣다** (to listen) and **걷다** (to walk). These are two of the most common ㄷ irregular verbs.

Unlike the ㅡ and **ㄹ irregular** rules, which only apply before **-아/어** endings, the ㅂ and **ㄷ irregular** rules apply before both **-아/어** and **-으** endings.

ㄷ irregular: ㄷ → ㄹ before -아/어, -으

듣다 → 들어요

듣 + -어요 → 들 + -어요 → **들어요**
└→ ㄷ changes to ㄹ before the vowel 어.

걷다 → 걸어요

걷 + -어요 → 걸 + -어요 → **걸어요**
└→ ㄷ changes to ㄹ before the vowel 어.

Not all ㄷ-ending verbs are irregular. Many keep the ㄷ and follow the regular rules, like **닫다** (to close) → **닫아요** and **믿다** (to believe) → **믿어요**. So just remember **듣다** and **걷다** as key examples of the ㄷ irregular rule.

UNIT 15

A/V-지요?

..., right?

Video 21

Let's briefly explore a useful expression for keeping a conversation going. You can use **-지요?** when you want to confirm something or seek agreement. It's like saying "right?", "isn't it?", or "don't you?". You can also use it to show interest in the other person or to gently express empathy. It's a way of saying, "I think I know, but I want to hear it from you."

CRACKING THE PATTERN CODE

The pattern is very simple. Just attach -지요? to the verb or adjective stem—no vowel or consonant change needed.

좋다 → 좋**지요**? It's good, **isn't it**?
[조치요]

쓰다 → 쓰**지요**? You're using it, **right**?

For **N**이에요/예요, use **N**이지요?/지요?

만 원이에요 → 만 원**이지요**? It's 10,000 won, **isn't it**?

의사예요 → 의사**지요**? You are a doctor, **aren't you**?

For the past tense, just add past tense ending -았/었- before -지요? You can think of it as using -았/었지요? instead of -았/었어요.

보다 → **봤어요** → **봤지요**? You saw it, **didn't you**?

피곤하다 → 피곤**했어요** → 피곤**했지요**? You were tired, **weren't you**?

Tip!
You'll also hear the shorter form **-죠?** in casual speech.

와인 wine • 쓰다 to use, to write • 만 원 [마눤] 10,000 won • 의사 doctor • 보다 to see/watch • 피곤하다 to be tired

CORE SENTENCES

MP3 42

바쁘다	오늘	바쁘	지요?	You're busy today, right?
좋아하다	커피	좋아하	지요?	You like coffee, right?
못 마시다	술을	못 마시	지요?	You can't drink alcohol, right?
듣다* → 들었어요	그 노래	들었	지요?	You listened to that song, didn't you?

Essential Practices

MP3 43

1. Change each sentence into the -지요? sentence to confirm or check.

(1) 한국 드라마를 좋아해요. → 한국 드라마를 좋아하지요? You like Korean dramas, right?

(2) 케이크가 맛있어요. → ______________? The cake is delicious, isn't it?

(3) 주말 잘 보냈어요? → ______________? You had a good weekend, right?

(4) 감기 걸렸어요? → ______________? You caught a cold, didn't you?

2. Complete each short dialogue using the -지요? pattern and the hint word.

(1) 좋다 to be good
A: 날씨가 좋지요? The weather is good, isn't it?
B: 네, 정말 좋아요! Yes, it really is!

(2) 바쁘다 to be busy
A: 오늘 ______________? You are busy today, right?
B: 아니요, 시간 있어요. No, I have time.

(3) 미국 사람이다 to be American
A: 제니 씨는 ______________? Jennie is American, isn't she?
B: 아니요, 뉴질랜드 사람이에요. No, she's a New Zealander.

(4) 안 먹다 not to eat
A: 알렉스 씨는 고기를 ______________? Alex doesn't eat meat, right?
B: 네, 안 먹어요. No, he doesn't.

Tip!

In Korean, answers to negative questions agree with the meaning of the sentence. For example, if someone asks "**안 바빠요?**" (You're not busy?), answering **네** means "Yes, that's right—I'm not busy." not "No."

UNIT 16

A/V-네요

Oh, it's ...

Video 22

-네요 is another useful expression that adds a conversational tone. It's used when you express a realization or feeling, or react to something new. You can also use it to agree with someone's impression or comment. It can translate to phrases like "Oh, it's...," "Wow," "really," or "certainly."

CRACKING THE PATTERN CODE

To form -네요, simply attach it to the verb or adjective stem. If the stem ends in ㄹ, drop the ㄹ before adding -네요.

싸다 → 싸네요 Oh, it's cheap.

덥다 → 덥네요 Oh, it's hot.

달다 → 다네요 Oh, it's sweet.

└→ drop the final consonant ㄹ

You can use -네요 both when **starting a conversation** and when **responding** to someone else. It's a great way to sound natural and engaged.

A: 와, 날씨가 **춥네요!** Oh, the weather is cold!

B: 네, 정말 **춥네요!** Yes, it really is!

For the past tense, just add -았/었- before -네요. You can think of it as using -았/었네요 instead of -았/었어요.

꽃이 피다 → 꽃이 **폈어요** → 꽃이 **폈네요!** Oh, the flowers have bloomed!

케이크 cake • 싸다 to be cheap • 덥다 (the weather) to be hot • 달다 to be sweet • 춥다 (the weather) to be cold • 꽃이 피다 for flowers to bloom

CORE SENTENCES

MP3 44

예쁘다	꽃이 **예쁘**	**네요!**	Wow, the flowers are pretty!
많다	과일이 **많**	**네요!**	There are so many fruits!
불다	바람이 **부**	**네요!**	Oh, the wind is blowing.
빠르다	인터넷이 **빠르**	**네요!**	Wow, the internet is fast!
닫다 → 닫았어요	식당이 일찍 **닫았**	**네요!**	Oh, the restaurant closed early.

Essential Practices

MP3 45

1. Change each sentence into the -네요 sentence to express your impression.

(1) 여기 커피가 싸요. → 여기 커피가 싸네요! Oh, the coffee here is cheap!

(2) 포도가 달아요. → ____________! Oh, the grapes are sweet!

(3) 인터넷이 빨라요.* → ____________! Wow, the internet is fast!

(4) 지수 씨가 일찍 일어났어요. → ____________! Oh, Jisoo got up early!

2. Complete the short dialogues using the hint words with the -네요 pattern.

(1) 예쁘다 to be pretty
A: 이 꽃 정말 ____________! This flower is really pretty!
B: 예쁘지요? 제 친구가 사 줬어요. Isn't it? My friend bought it for me.

(2) 덥다 to be hot
A: 날씨가 너무 덥지요? The weather is too hot, right?
B: 네, 정말 ____________. Yes, it's really hot.

(3) 배부르다 to be full
A: 너무 ____________. Oh, I'm so full!
B: 맞아요. 진짜 배불러요. Right. I'm really full too.

(4) 크다 to be big
A: 와, 백화점이 ____________! Wow, this department store is huge!
B: 네, 진짜 커요! Yes, it really is!

UNIT 17

Ready to Make A/V Patterns ②: -(으) Ending

형용사 / 동사 패턴 만들기 준비 ② : -(으) 어미

Video 23

We've seen lots of patterns so far—many of them used the **-아/어** ending, and some didn't, like **-이에요/예요**, **-네요**, or **-지요?**. This time, let's learn how to use another important ending: **-(으)**. This ending is used in many patterns like **-(으)세요**, **-(으)ㄹ 거예요**, or **-(으)ㄴ데요**, so understanding how it works will really help!

❶ Key Points of -(으) Ending

When a pattern begins with -(으), you need to decide whether to **keep** 으 or **skip** it. That's why (으) is written in parentheses—it's sometimes there, and sometimes not, depending on the stem it's attached to.

It all depends on whether the stem ends in a final consonant (받침) or not.

보다 (stem: 보)   먹다 (stem: 먹)   만들다 (stem: 만들)

Here are the general rules.

1 If the stem ends in a consonant (받침) → Keep -으.

받침 (O)
닫다 (stem) + -으 → 닫으

2 If the stem ends in a vowel (no 받침) → Skip -으.

받침 (X)
보다 (stem) + X → 보

3 If the stem ends in ㄹ 받침 → Drop ㄹ and treat it like it has no 받침.

ㄹ받침
놀다 (stem) + X → 노

② Making Patterns with -(으)

To see how patterns with the -(으) ending work, let's take -(으)세요 as an example. The easiest way is to start by preparing two forms: **one with** -으 and **one without it**.

-(으)세요 → -으세요 or -세요

Then, based on the stem, choose the right one.

Word	Stem	Check 받침		Pattern Shape		-(으)세요 Form
닫다 to close	닫	○	+	-으세요	→	닫으세요
고르다 to choose	고르	×	+	-세요	→	고르세요
살다 to live	살 → 사	×	+	-세요	→	사세요

Now let's try another pattern: -(으)ㄴ데요. Again, prepare two forms first.

-(으)ㄴ데요 → -은데요 or -ㄴ데요

Here's how this works with some example words:

Word	Stem	Check 받침		Pattern Shape		-(으)ㄴ데요 Form
좋다 to be good	좋	○	+	-은데요	→	좋은데요
예쁘다 to be pretty	예쁘	×	+	-ㄴ데요	→	예쁜데요
멀다 to be far	멀 → 머	×	+	-ㄴ데요	→	먼데요

As you see in the case of 예쁜데요 and 먼데요, when the stem ends in a vowel, the first consonant of the pattern, like ㄴ in -ㄴ데요, **slides into the 받침 position** at the end of the stem.

예쁘- + -ㄴ데요 → **예쁜**데요
stem

Remember how Korean syllables are built? They follow the **C + V** or **C + V + C structure**. A consonant can't form a syllable by itself, so it moves to the end of the stem to complete a smooth Korean syllable.

☑ Self-Check

1. **Complete the table for -(으)세요.**

-(으)세요 → ____________ or ____________

Word	Stem	Check 받침	Pattern Shape	-(으)세요 Form
받다 to receive		+	→	
사다 to buy		+	→	
만들다 to make		+	→	

2. **Complete the table for -(으)ㄴ데요.**

-(으)ㄴ데요 → ____________ or ____________

Word	Stem	Check 받침	Pattern Shape	-(으)ㄴ데요 Form
작다 to be small		+	→	
크다 to be big		+	→	
달다 to be sweet		+	→	

[Answer Key]

1. -(으)세요 → -으세요 or -세요
   받다 → 받 (◯) + -으세요 → 받으세요 **사다** → 사 (X) + -세요 → 사세요 **만들다** → 만들 → 만드 (X) + -세요 → 만드세요
2. -(으)ㄴ데요 → -은데요 or -ㄴ데요
   작다 → 작 (◯) + -은데요 → 작은데요 **크다** → 크 (X) + -ㄴ데요 → 큰데요 **달다** → 달 → 다 (X) + -ㄴ데요 → 단데요

3 Wrap-up: Summary of -(으) Rules

Let's review what you've learned:

- Patterns that begin with -(으) have two forms: one **with** -으, and one **without it**.
- If the stem ends in **a consonant** (받침), use the form **with** -으.
- If the stem ends in **a vowel** (no 받침) or ㄹ **받침** (drop ㄹ), use the form **without** -으.

☑ Self-Check

1. Fill in the table by choosing the correct form of the pattern -(으)ㄹ까요?. If you already have the steps in your head, feel free to skip them and write only the completed form.

-(으)ㄴ데요 → ________ or ________

Word	Stem	Check 받침	Pattern Shape	-(으)ㄹ까요? Form
닫다			+	→
좋다			+	→
고르다			+	→
예쁘다			+	→
살다			+	→
멀다			+	→

[Answer Key] 1. -(으)ㄹ까요? → -을까요? or -ㄹ까요?
닫다 → 닫 (◯) + -을까요? → 닫을까요? **좋다** → 좋 (◯) + -을까요? → 좋을까요?
고르다 → 고르 (✕) + -ㄹ까요? → 고를까요?
예쁘다 → 예쁘 (✕) + -ㄹ까요? → 예쁠까요? **살다** → 살 → 사 (✕) + -ㄹ까요? → 살까요?
멀다 → 멀 → 머 (✕) + -ㄹ까요? → 멀까요?

UNIT 18

V-(으)세요

Please V (command)

Video 24

V-(으)세요 is an informal polite command pattern used to give directions or suggest actions. You'll often see it in everyday contexts like public signs, giving directions, or recipes. In fact, you've already heard phrases like **안녕히 가세요**, **안녕히 계세요**, and **맛있게 드세요**!

CRACKING THE PATTERN CODE

The -아/어요 form can be used for casual commands, but -(으)세요 is more polite and respectful. The -(으)세요 form comes from combining the **honorific ending** -(으)시- and the **polite ending** -어요. Over time, these merged into the form we use today: -(으)세요.

→ honorific ending
-(으)시- + -어요 → -(으)셔요 → **-(으)세요**
→ polite ending

To decide between -으세요 and -세요, look at the final sound of the verb stem. If the stem ends in a consonant (except ㄹ), use -으세요. If the stem ends in a vowel or ends in ㄹ, drop the ㄹ and use -세요.

받침 ○ + **-으세요**

앉다 → 앉 + **-으세요** → **앉으세요** [안즈세요]
→ ends in ㄵ (받침 ○)

받침 ×, ㄹ + **-세요**

가다 → 가 + **-세요** → **가세요**
→ ends in ㅏ (받침 ×)

열다 → 여 + **-세요** → **여세요**
→ ends in ㄹ, so drop ㄹ

여기 here • 드시다 to eat/drink (honorific) • 주무시다 to sleep (honorific) • 말씀하시다 to say (honorific) • 계시다 to stay/be somewhere (honorific)

• **Common Honorific Verbs:** Some verbs have special honorific forms instead of using -(으)세요.

먹어요 / 마셔요 → 드세요
먹다 to eat, 마시다 to drink

자요 → 주무세요
자다 to sleep

말해요 → 말씀하세요
말하다 to say

있어요 ↔ 계세요
있다 to be (somewhere)

Tip!
The word **있어요** has two honorific forms. Use **있으세요** for "have/has" and **계세요** for "am/are/is somewhere."

CORE SENTENCES

MP3 46

씻다	손을 자주	씻으세요.	Wash your hands often.
주다	영수증	주세요.	Please give me the receipt.
가다	이쪽으로	가세요.	Go this way.
기다리다	잠깐	기다리세요.	Please wait.
열다	문을	여세요.	Please open the door.
먹다	이 약을	드세요.	Please take this medicine.
마시다	물을 많이	드세요.	Please drink a lot of water.
자다	일찍	주무세요.	Please go to bed early.
말하다	이름을	말씀하세요.	Please say your name.
있다	안녕히	계세요.	Stay in peace. (=Good bye.)

Essential Practices

MP3 47

1. Convert the given verb into the -(으)세요 form and read it aloud.

씻다 → 씻으세요 to wash	앉다 → ______ to sit	벗다 → ______ to take off
가다 → ______ to go	보다 → ______ to see/watch	기다리다 → ______ to wait
열다 → ______ to open	걸다 → ______ to hang	자다 → ______ to sleep
마시다 → ______ to drink	말하다 → ______ to speak	있다 → ______ to be (somewhere)

2. Complete the sentences using the hint word and the -(으)세요 pattern.

(1) 앉다 to sit

Please sit here.

→ 여기 ______________.

(2) 씻다 to wash

Please wash your hands.

→ 손을 ______________.

(3) 벗다 to take off

Please take off your shoes.

→ 신발을 ______________.

(4) 조용히 하다 to be quiet

Shh, please be quiet.

→ 쉿, ______________.

(5) 걸다 to hang

Please hang your clothes here.

→ 여기에 옷을 ______________.

3. **Complete the dialogues using the hint words. Then read them aloud.**

(1) 마시다

A: 이 주스 ____드세요____. Please drink this juice.

B: 와, 감사합니다. Wow, thank you.

(2) 주다
기다리다

A: 어서 오세요. 뭐 드릴까요? Welcome! May I take your order?

B: 김치찌개 ______________. Kimchi jjigae, please.

A: 네, 잠깐만 ______________. Sure, please wait a moment.

(3) 먹다
자다

A: 감기에 걸렸어요. 약 있어요? I caught a cold. Do you have any medicine?

B: 아이고, 이 약 ______________. Oh no, take this medicine.
그리고 푹 ______________. And sleep well.

A: 감사해요. Thank you.

(4) 타다
가다

A: 서울역에 어떻게 가요? How can I get to Seoul Station?

B: 지하철을 ______________. 지하철이 빨라요. Take the subway. The subway is fast.

A: 지하철역이 어디에 있어요? Where is the subway station?

B: 이쪽으로 ______________. Please go this way.

A: 감사합니다! Thank you!

EXPLORE FURTHER

A/V-(으)세요 for Questions and Honorific Statements

We've practiced using **-(으)세요** with verbs to make polite commands. But because it includes the honorific ending **-(으)시-**, you can also use it to ask questions or make polite statements! In these cases, you can use **-(으)세요** with adjectives as well.

Honorifics are usually used for someone older or of higher status. But they're also common when talking to people you're not close with—like store staff, coworkers, or customers.

1 Asking Polite Questions with -(으)세요?

You can use the **A/V-(으)세요?** pattern to ask polite, respectful questions.

바쁘세요? Are you busy? (to the listener, using the honorific)

엄마가 바쁘세요? Is Mom busy? (about a respected third person)

2 Making Honorific Statements about Someone Else

When the subject is a third person (not the listener), **-(으)세요** is not a command. It becomes a polite statement that shows respect for the person you're talking about.

이쪽으로 가세요. Go this way. (command to the listener)

엄마가 회사에 가세요. Mom is going to work. (polite statement about Mom)

UNIT 19

V-지 마세요

(Please) Do not V

Video 25

We've learned how to use the **-(으)세요** pattern to give polite commands or directions. Equally important is knowing how to politely tell someone not to do something. The pattern **V-지 마세요** is a key way to make polite requests or instructions not to do something.

CRACKING THE PATTERN CODE

Regardless of whether the verb stem ends in a consonant or a vowel, simply attach **-지 마세요** to the stem.

먹다 → 먹**지 마세요** (Please) don't eat ~

하다 → 하**지 마세요** (Please) don't do ~

열다 → 열**지 마세요** (Please) don't open ~

The pattern V-지 마세요 is formed by combining the basic form V-지 말다 with the command pattern -(으)세요.

V-지 말다 → V-지 마 + **-세요** → **V-지 마세요**

└→ ends in ㄹ, so drop ㄹ

Tip!

V-지 말다 is used exclusively for commands **-지 마세요** (Please don't ~) or suggestions **-지 말아요** (Let's not ~).

사진을 찍다 to take a photo

CORE SENTENCES

MP3 48

먹다	음식을 **먹**	지 마세요.	Please do not eat food.
나가다	밖에 **나가**	지 마세요.	Don't go outside.
걱정하다	**걱정하**	지 마세요.	Don't worry.
열다	창문을 **열**	지 마세요.	Please don't open the window.
피우다	여기에서 담배를 **피우**	지 마세요.	Don't smoke here.

Essential Practices

MP3 49

1. Change each sentence from -(으)세요 to -지 마세요.

(1) 앉다 to sit — 여기 앉으세요. ↔ 여기 앉지 마세요 . Please don't sit here.

(2) 뛰다 to jump/run — 뛰세요. ↔ ________. Please don't jump/run here.

(3) 타다 to get on (vehicles) — 택시를 타세요. ↔ 택시를 ________. Please don't take a taxi.

(4) 걸다 to hang — 여기에 옷을 거세요. ↔ 여기에 옷을 ________. Please don't hang clothes here.

2. Complete the dialogues using the hint words. Then read them aloud.

(1) **먹다**
A: 이 빵 먹어도 돼요? Can I eat this bread?
B: 아니요, ________. 오래됐어요. No, don't eat it. It's old.

(2) **사다**
A: 이거 살까요? Should I buy this?
B: 아니요, ________. 너무 비싸요. No, don't buy it. It's too expensive.

(3) **피우다**
A: 여기에서 담배 피워도 돼요? Can I smoke here?
B: 안 돼요. ________. No, don't smoke.

(4) **나가다 걱정하다**
A: 비가 많이 와요. ________. It's raining a lot. Don't go out.
B: 괜찮아요. ________. It's okay. Don't worry.

UNIT 20

V-(으)ㄹ까요?

Shall we ~? / Should I ~?

Video 26

V-(으)ㄹ까요? is used to ask for someone's opinion—either about doing something together, or about whether the speaker should do something. In English, it can correspond to "Shall we...?" for making a suggestion, and "Shall I...?" or "Should I...?" when asking for advice or permission.

CRACKING THE PATTERN CODE

The pattern -(으)ㄹ까요? has two forms: -을까요? and -ㄹ까요?. To choose the right one, look at the final sound of the stem.

받침 O	+ -을까요?	닫다 → 닫 + -을까요? → 닫을까요? ↳ ends in ㄷ (받침 O)
받침 X, ㄹ	+ -ㄹ까요?	가다 → 가 + -ㄹ까요? → 갈까요? ↳ ends in ㅏ (받침 X)
		만들다 → 만드 + -ㄹ까요? → 만들까요? ↳ ends in ㄹ, so drop ㄹ

Keep in mind that -(으)ㄹ까요? is not used to make statements. Depending on the situation, different response patterns are used.

A: 우리 카페에 **갈까요?** Shall we go to a café?
B: 네, **가요.** Yes, let's go.

A: 창문을 **열까요?** Should I open the window?
B: 네, **여세요.** Yes, please open it.

Tip!

You can also use -(으)ㄹ까요? to ask what someone thinks will happen. It's like saying "Do you think...?" in English. In this case, adjectives can be used too. For example: **내일 추울까요?** (Do you think it will be cold tomorrow?)

만들다 to make • 카페 café

• **Similar expression: -(으)ㄹ래요? (Would you like to ~?)**

-(으)ㄹ래요? can be used to make a suggestion or ask about the other person's preference. Unlike -(으)ㄹ까요?, which is only used for questions, -(으)ㄹ래요? can also be used in answers to express the speaker's own intention.

A: 같이[가치] 커피 **마실래요?** Would you like to have coffee together?

B: 네, **마실래요.** Yes, I'd like to have some.

CORE SENTENCES

MP3 50

찍다	같이 사진	**찍을**	까요?	Shall we take a photo together?
먹다	우리 밥	**먹을**	까요?	Shall we have a meal?
하다	뭐	**할**	까요?	What shall we/I do?
가져가다	우산을	**가져갈**	까요?	Shall I take an umbrella with me?
만나다	언제	**만날**	까요?	When shall we meet?
도와드리다	제가	**도와드릴**	까요?	Shall I help you?
열다	창문을	**열**	까요?	Should I open the window?
만들다	무슨 음식을	**만들**	까요?	What kind of food should we/I make?
굽다*	쿠키를	**구울**	까요?	Shall we/I bake cookies?
걷다*	좀	**걸을**	까요?	Shall we walk a little?

* irregular form (ㅂ → 우, ㄷ → ㄹ)

Essential Practices

MP3 51

1. Change each verb into the -(으)ㄹ까요? form and say it out loud.

사진 찍다 → 사진 찍을까요?
to take a photo

먹다 → ____________
to eat

닫다 → ____________
to close

쇼핑하다 → ____________
to shop

가져가다 → ____________
to take (with someone)

만나다 → ____________
to meet

열다 → ____________
to open

팔다 → ____________
to sell

만들다 → ____________
to make

굽다* → ____________
to bake/grill

돕다* → ____________
to help

듣다* → ____________
to listen

2. Look at the situations and complete each conversation using the correct -(으)ㄹ까요? form. Use each word in the box only once.

먹다	가져가다	도와드리다	찍다	열다	걷다*	굽다*	듣다*

(1) You and your friend are hungry, so you suggest eating together.

A: 우리 밥 먹을까요? Shall we eat?

B: 네, 밥 먹어요! Yes, let's eat!

(2) You want to take a photo with your friend, so you suggest it.

A: 우리 사진 ____________? Shall we take a picture?

B: 좋아요. 찍어요! Great, let's take one!

(3) Your teacher is carrying something heavy. You want to offer help.

A: 선생님, 제가 좀 ____________? Shall I help you?

B: 아니에요, 괜찮아요. 고마워요! It's okay, thank you!

(4) It's hot, so you ask if you should open the window.

A: 여기 좀 덥네요. 창문을 ____________? It's a bit hot in here. Should I open the window?

B: 네, 열어 주세요. Yes, please do.

(5) Your friend is visiting your house. You want to suggest baking cookies together.

A: 쿠키 좋아하지요? 같이 쿠키 ________________? You like cookies, right? Shall we bake cookies?

B: 좋아요! Sounds great!

(6) You're getting ready to go out and wonder if you should take an umbrella.

A: 우산을 ________________? Should I take an umbrella?

B: 네, 가져가세요. 비가 올 거예요. Yes, take it with you. It's going to rain.

(7) You want to listen to music together, so you suggest it.

A: 같이 노래 ________________? Shall we listen to music?

B: 좋아요. 무슨 노래 좋아해요? Sure! What kind of music do you like?

(8) You ate a big meal with your friend. You feel very full.

A: 와, 너무 배부르네요. Wow, I feel really full.

B: 진짜 배불러요. 우리 좀 ________________? Yeah, me too. Shall we walk a little?

A: 좋아요. 공원에 갈까요? Good idea. Shall we go to the park?

EXPLORE FURTHER

Quick Reminder: Irregular Rules

So far, we've looked at four common irregular rules. These patterns happen when certain verb or adjective stems end in a specific final consonant or vowel: ㅡ, 르, ㄷ, and ㅂ.

The ㅡ and 르 rules only apply before **-아/어**, but the ㄷ and ㅂ rules apply before **both -아/어 and -으**.

- **ㅡ irregular**: ㅡ disappears before -아/어. (always) e.g. 쓰다 → 써요
- **르 irregular**: 르 becomes ㄹㄹ before -아/어. (almost always, 99%!) e.g. 빠르다 → 빨라요
- **ㄷ irregular**: ㄷ changes to ㄹ before -아/어 and -으. (some words) e.g. 걷다 → 걸어요, 걷다 → 걸을까요?
- **ㅂ irregular**: ㅂ changes to 우 before -아/어 and -으. (some words) e.g. 굽다 → 구워요 / 구울까요?

These are the four main irregulars in this book. Other irregulars include: ㄹ irregular (ㄹ drops before ㄴ, ㅂ, ㅅ), ㅅ irregular (ㅅ disappears before -아/어, -으), and ㅎ irregular (ㅎ disappears before -아/어, -으). We won't cover them in detail, but feel free to check them out later.

UNIT 21

A/V-(으)ㄹ 거예요

will A/V

Video 27

We've studied the present tense **-아/어요** and past tense **-았/었어요**. Now it's time to learn about the future tense! **-(으)ㄹ 거예요** is similar to "will" or "am/are/is going to" in English. Just like English "will," **-(으)ㄹ 거예요** expresses a future plan, intention, prediction, or guess.

CRACKING THE PATTERN CODE

The pattern -(으)ㄹ 거예요 has two forms: -을 거예요 and -ㄹ 거예요. To choose the right one, look at the final sound of the verb stem.

받침 ○	+ -을 거예요	먹다 → 먹 + -을 거예요 → 먹을 거예요 └→ ends in ㄱ (받침 ○)
받침 ×, ㄹ	+ -ㄹ 거예요	가다 → 가 + -ㄹ 거예요 → 갈 거예요 └→ ends in ㅏ (받침 ×)
		만들다 → 만드 + -ㄹ 거예요 → 만들 거예요 └→ ends in ㄹ, so drop ㄹ

Note that 거예요 is pronounced tensed as [꺼예요] due to the influence of the ㄹ 받침 sound.

먹을 거예요	갈 거예요	만들 거예요
[머글 꺼예요]	[갈 꺼예요]	[만들 꺼예요]

You can also use -(으)ㄹ 거예요 to express predictions or assumptions, as if you're saying "I think..." or "I guess..." in English.

바람이 **불 거예요.** *(I think)* it will be windy.

치킨을 **먹을 거예요.** 정말 **맛있을 거예요!** I'll eat chicken. *(I think)* it'll be really delicious!

치킨 fried chicken • 바람이 불다 for wind to blow

Use -(으)ㄹ 거예요? when asking about someone's plans or intentions. But if you want to ask what someone thinks or guesses, don't use -(으)ㄹ 거예요?. Instead, use -(으)ㄹ까요?.

A: 내일 뭐 **할 거예요**? What are you going to do tomorrow?
B: 공부할 거예요. I'm going to study. (a plan)

A: 비가 **올까요**? Do you think it will rain?
B: 네, 비가 올 거예요. Yes, (I think) it will rain.

Tip!

-(으)ㄹ 거예요 can sometimes describe what the speaker assumes is happening right now, like **지금** 밖에 바람이 **불 거예요**. (I think the wind is blowing outside now.)

CORE SENTENCES

MP3 52

하다	주말에 뭐	**할**	거예요? What are you going to do on the weekend?
읽다	책을	**읽을**	거예요. I will read a book.
만들다	빵을	**만들**	거예요. I will make some bread.
만나다	친구를	**만날**	거예요. I will meet a friend.
오다	비가	**올**	거예요. It will rain.
많다	사람이	**많을**	거예요. There will be many people.
끝나다	수업이 곧	**끝날**	거예요. The class will finish soon.
듣다*	음악을	**들을**	거예요. I will listen to music.
춥다*	날씨가	**추울**	거예요. The weather will be cold.
어렵다*	시험이	**어려울**	거예요. The test will be difficult.

* irregular form (ㄷ → ㄹ, ㅂ → 우)

Essential Practices

MP3 53

1. Complete the table by writing the present, past, and future forms of each word.

Basic Form	Present Tense -아/어요	Past Tense -았/었어요	Future Plan, Guess -(으)ㄹ 거예요
하다 to do	해요		할 거예요
읽다 to read		읽었어요	
만들다 to make	만들어요		
불다 to blow	불어요		
만나다 to meet		만났어요	
듣다* to listen	들어요		
걷다* to walk		걸었어요	
굽다* to bake/grill	구워요		
쉽다* to be easy		쉬웠어요	

2. Complete the sentences using the hint word and the -(으)ㄹ 거예요 pattern.

(1) 가다 to go

Where are you going on the weekend?

→ 주말에 어디 ____갈 거예요____?

(2) 입다 to wear

What will you wear tomorrow?

→ 내일 뭐 ____________?

(3) 읽다 to read

What kind of book are you going to read?

→ 무슨 책을 ____________?

(4) 배우다 to learn

I am going to learn French.

→ 프랑스어를 ____________.

(5) 오다 to come

It will snow.

→ 눈이 ____________.

(6) 불다 to blow

It will be very windy.

→ 바람이 많이 ____________.

(7) 끝나다 to end

The movie will finish soon.

→ 영화가 곧 ____________.

3. Complete the dialogues using the hint words.

(1) 안 오다 / 불다

A: 날씨가 춥네요. 눈이 올까요? The weather is cold. Do you think it will snow?

B: 아니요, ___안 올 거예요___. 제가 뉴스를 봤어요. No, it won't. I saw the news.

하지만 바람이 많이 ___불 거예요___. But it'll be very windy.

(2) 운동하다 / 쉬다

A: 저녁에 ______________? Are you going to work out this evening?

B: 아니요, 오늘은 안 해요. 집에서 ______________. No, not today. I'll rest at home.

(3) 사다 / 굽다*

A: 어디 가세요? Where are you going?

B: 마트에 가요. I'm going to the supermarket.

A: 오! 뭐 ______________? Oh! What are you going to buy?

B: 밀가루요. 쿠키를 ______________. Flour. I'm going to bake some cookies.

(4) 하다 / 배우다 / 재미있다

A: 방학 때 뭐 ______________? What will you do over the vacation?

B: 스페인어를 ______________. I'm going to learn Spanish.

A: 오! 스페인어 공부 좋네요. Oh! Studying Spanish sounds great.

B: 네, ______________! Yes, I think it will be fun!

EXPLORE FURTHER

Another Way to Say "I will ~": V-(으)ㄹ게요

Use **V-(으)ㄹ게요** when you want to show your decision or make a promise directly to the listener. The key difference from **-(으)ㄹ 거예요** is who you're speaking to and why—whether it's simply a plan or a promise.

A/V-(으)ㄹ 거예요 → Expressing a plan or prediction (future statement)

V-(으)ㄹ게요 → Expressing a decision or promise (listener involvement)

Use **V-(으)ㄹ게요** when you decide to do something right now, or when you're making a promise to the person you're speaking with. It shows listener involvement and can't be used for general predictions or plans. For those, you should use **-(으)ㄹ 거예요** instead.

A: 알렉스 씨, 제 메시지 봤어요? Alex, did you read my message?

B: 아, 아직 못 봤어요. 지금 **볼게요**. Oh, I couldn't read it yet. I'll check it now—I promise.
[볼께요]

A: 내일 뭐 할 거예요? What are you going to do tomorrow?

B: 영화를 **볼 거예요**. I'll watch a movie tomorrow. (=just a plan)
[볼 꺼예요]

In the **-(으)ㄹ게요** pattern, **게요** is pronounced **[께요]** because of the **ㄹ** at the end of the verb stem.

UNIT 22

V-(으)ㄹ 수 있어요

can V

Video 28

The pattern -(으)ㄹ 수 있어요 means "can" in English. You can use it to talk about what someone is able to do or what is possible in a situation. As you practice, try thinking of different situations where it's used—from saying what you can do, to asking about availability, schedules, or whether something is allowed.

CRACKING THE PATTERN CODE

The pattern -(으)ㄹ 수 있어요 has two forms: -을 수 있어요 and -ㄹ 수 있어요. To choose the right one, look at the final sound of the verb stem.

받침 O + -을 수 있어요

먹다 → 먹 + -을 수 있어요 → 먹을 수 있어요
↳ ends in ㄱ (받침 O)

받침 X, ㄹ + -ㄹ 수 있어요

쓰다 → 쓰 + -ㄹ 수 있어요 → 쓸 수 있어요
↳ ends in ㅡ (받침 X)

불다 → 부 + -ㄹ 수 있어요 → 불 수 있어요
↳ ends in ㄹ, so drop ㄹ

Note that 수 is pronounced strongly as [쑤] due to the influence of the ㄹ 받침 sound.

먹을 수 있어요	쓸 수 있어요	불 수 있어요
[머글 쑤 이써요]	[쓸 쑤 이써요]	[불 쑤 이써요]

To say "cannot," you can use V-(으)ㄹ 수 없어요 or 못 V-아/어요. The 못 pattern is more commonly used in everyday conversation, while V-(으)ㄹ 수 없어요 sounds a bit more formal.

먹을 수 있어요 ↔ 먹을 수 없어요 = 못 먹어요
can eat — cannot eat

불다 to blow

The basic form of this pattern is -(으)ㄹ 수 있다. Try using it with different endings to make new expressions, like -(으)ㄹ 수 있었어요 (was able to), -(으)ㄹ 수 있을 거예요 (will probably be able to), and so on.

Tip!

There's another expression, **-(으)ㄹ 줄 알다/모르다**, which is similar to **-(으)ㄹ 수 있다/없다**. It literally means "to know how to do something / not to know how to do something." It only expresses ability or skill, not possibility.

CORE SENTENCES

MP3 54

읽다	한국어를	**읽을**	수 있어요. I can read Korean.
쓰다	한글로 이름을	**쓸**	수 있어요. I can write my name in Hangeul.
타다	자전거를	**탈**	수 있어요. I can ride a bike.
만나다	내일	**만날**	수 있어요? Can we meet tomorrow?
부르다	한국 노래를	**부를**	수 있어요. I can sing a Korean song.
만들다	김밥을	**만들**	수 있어요. I can make gimbap.
입어 보다	이거	**입어 볼**	수 있어요? Can I try this on?

먹다 Q. 매운 음식 **먹을** 수 있어요? Can you eat spicy food?

A. 네, 먹을 수 있어요. Yes, I can. / 아니요, 못 먹어요. = 먹을 수 없어요. No, I can't.

불다 Q. 하모니카 **불** 수 있어요? Can you play the harmonica?

A. 네, 불 수 있어요. Yes, I can. / 아니요, 못 불어요. = 불 수 없어요. No, I can't.

수영하다 Q. **수영할** 수 있어요? Can you swim?

A. 네, (수영)할 수 있어요. Yes, I can. / 아니요, (수영) 못 해요. = (수영)할 수 없어요. No, I can't.

Tip!

When you answer a question with a **noun + 하다 verb** like **수영하다** (to swim), you don't need to repeat the noun in the answer. Just say **할 수 있어요, 못 해요** or **할 수 없어요**.

Essential Practices

MP3 55

1. Complete the table by writing the appropriate forms of each word.

Basic Form	V-(으)ㄹ 수 있어요	V-(으)ㄹ 수 없어요	못 V-아/어요
운전하다 to drive	운전할 수 있어요	운전할 수 없어요	운전 못 해요
운동하다 to exercise			
만나다 to meet			
읽다 to read			
만들다 to make			
걷다* to walk			못 걸어요
굽다* to bake/grill		구울 수 없어요	

2. Complete each conversation using the hint words and -(으)ㄹ 수 있어요 and 못 -아/어요.

(1) 입어 보다 to try on
A: 실례합니다. 이 옷 ___입어 볼 수 있어요___? Excuse me, can I try this on?
B: 네, 그럼요. Yes, of course.

(2) 불다 to blow
A: 하모니카 ______________? Can you play the harmonica?
B: 아니요, ___못 불어요___. No, I can't.

(3) 쓰다 to write
A: 한글로 이름 ______________? Can you write your name in Hangeul?
B: 네, ______________. Yes, I can.

(4) 타다 to ride
A: 자전거 ______________? Can you ride a bike?
B: 아니요, ______________. No, I can't.

(5) 만나다 to meet
A: 우리 내일 ______________? Can we meet tomorrow?
B: 아, 미안해요. 내일은 약속이 있어요. Sorry, I have plans tomorrow.

(6) 먹다 to eat
A: 매운 음식 ______________? Can you eat spicy food?
B: 아니요, ______________. No, I can't.

(7) 부르다 to sing a song A: 한국 노래 ____________________? Can you sing a Korean song?

B: 네, ____________________! Yes, I can!

A: 와! 불러 주세요! Wow! Please sing for me!

(8) 놀다 to hang out A: 오늘 같이 ____________________? Can we hang out today?

B: 네, 시간 돼요! ____________________. Yes, I'm free! I can hang out.

(9) 수영하다 to swim A: ____________________? Can you swim?

B: 그럼요, ____________________! Of course, I can!

A: 와, 부러워요. 저는 수영을 ____________. Wow, I envy you. I can't swim.

EXPLORE FURTHER

V-아/어 주실 수 있어요? (Could you please ...?)

In everyday conversation, you can use **V-아/어 주실 수 있어요?** to politely ask for help or a favor. It's made by combining **-아/어 주시다** with **-(으)ㄹ 수 있어요?**.

-아/어 주시다 + **-(으)ㄹ 수 있어요?** → **-아/어 주실 수 있어요?**
└→ basic form of -아/어 주세요

This form is softer and more polite than simply saying **V-아/어 주세요**. It is commonly used when speaking to a stranger, a colleague, or someone older (e.g., in a restaurant, hotel, or airport).

이것 좀 **도와주실 수 있어요**? Could you help me with this?

방을 좀 **바꿔 주실 수 있어요**? Could you change the room? - e.g., in a hotel

When asking a friend or someone close to you for a favor, you can drop the honorific ending **-(으)시-** and use **-아/어 줄 수 있어요**? instead.

민수 씨, 이것 좀 **도와줄 수 있어요**? Minsu, can you help me with this?

알렉스 씨, 창문 좀 **열어 줄 수 있어요**? Alex, can you open the window?

UNIT
23 V-고 싶어요
I want to V

Video 29

When you want to say what you want to do, use the pattern **-고 싶어요**. This corresponds to "want to + verb" in English. You can use it in many everyday situations—when ordering food, making plans with a friend, or just saying how you feel in the moment.

CRACKING THE PATTERN CODE

The pattern -고 싶어요 is very simple to use. Just attach -고 싶어요 to the verb stem! It doesn't matter whether the verb ends in a consonant or vowel.

먹다 → 먹고 싶어요　　보다 → 보고 싶어요　　놀다 → 놀고 싶어요

Usually, the object of the verb uses 을/를. But with -고 싶어요, you usually use 이/가 to express strong emotions or longing.

영화(를) 보고 싶어요. I want to watch a movie.
(을/를 is used and can be dropped)

영화가 보고 싶어요. I want to watch a movie (very much).
(이/가 adds emotional emphasis.)

With people, ~이/가 보고 싶어요 means "I miss ~." You don't use the marker 을/를 here.

친구가 보고 싶어요. I miss my friend.

커피 coffee • 놀다 to play, to hang out

The basic form of -고 싶어요 is -고 싶다. To say "don't want to," you can use 안 **V**-고 싶어요 or **V**-고 싶지 않아요.

커피 마시고 싶어요 ↔ 커피 안 마시고 싶어요 = 커피 마시고 싶지 않아요

I want to have coffee. / I don't want to have coffee. [아나요]

Tip!

When talking about what someone else wants to do (third person), use -**고 싶어 해요**. For example: **저는 커피를 마시고 싶어요. 마크 씨는 콜라를 마시고 싶어 해요.** (I want to drink coffee. Mark wants to drink cola.)

CORE SENTENCES

MP3 56

먹다	라면	**먹**	고 싶어요.	I want to eat ramyeon.
읽다	책	**읽**	고 싶어요.	I want to read a book.
듣다	음악	**듣**	고 싶어요.	I want to listen to music.
가다	집에	**가**	고 싶어요.	I want to go home.
쉬다		**쉬**	고 싶어요.	I want to rest.
마시다	물을 좀	**마시**	고 싶어요.	I want to drink some water.
배우다	한국어를	**배우**	고 싶어요.	I want to learn Korean.
산책하다		**산책하**	고 싶어요.	I want to take a walk.
입어 보다	이 옷	**입어 보**	고 싶어요.	I want to try this on.
보다	친구가	**보**	고 싶어요.	I miss my friend.

Essential Practices

MP3 57

1. Change each verb into the -고 싶어요 form and say it out loud.

걷다 → 걷고 싶어요
to walk

읽다 → ____________
to read

닫다 → ____________
to close

쇼핑하다 → ____________
to shop

사다 → ____________
to buy

만나다 → ____________
to meet

입어 보다 → ____________
to try on

배우다 → ____________
to learn

돕다 → ____________
to help

2. Complete each sentence using -고 싶어요 or -고 싶지 않아요 to match the English meaning. Use the hint words in parentheses.

(1) I *want to* eat gimbap. = 김밥 먹고 싶어요.
(먹다, 김밥)

(2) I *don't want to* watch that movie. = 저 영화 보고 싶지 않아요.
(보다, 저 영화)

(3) I *don't want to* study today. = 오늘은 ____________.
(공부하다)

(4) I *want to* exercise. = ____________.
(운동하다)

(5) I *want to* drink juice. = ______ ____________.
(마시다, 주스)

(6) I *don't want to* buy this book. = ______ ____________.
(사다, 이 책)

(7) I *want to* try on that shirt. = ______ ____________.
(입어 보다, 저 셔츠)

(8) I *miss* my family. = ______ ____________.
(보다, 가족)

(9) I *don't want to* listen to music. = ______ ____________.
(듣다, 음악)

3. **Read the situations and complete each conversation using the -고 싶어요 pattern. Use each word in the box only once.**

~~쉬다~~	먹다	보다	배우다	마시다	여행하다	사다

(1) You're tired and want to rest.

A: 너무 피곤해요. 조금 ___쉬고 싶어요___. I'm so tired. I want to rest a bit.

B: 그래요. 푹 쉬세요! Okay. Get some good rest!

(2) You're talking about your vacation plans.

A: 방학에 뭐 할 거예요? What are you going to do during the vacation?

B: 저는 일본어를 ______________________. I want to learn Japanese.

A: 오, 그래요? 저는 스페인어를 배울 거예요. Oh, you do? I'm going to learn Spanish.

(3) You're traveling and feel hungry.

A: 배고파요. 뭐 좀 ______________________. I'm hungry. I want to eat something.

B: 식당에 갈까요? Should we go to a restaurant?

(4) You're shopping with your friend and see something you like.

A: 이 가방 예쁘네요. 이거 ______________________. This bag is pretty. I want to buy this.

B: 사세요! 오늘 세일이에요. Buy it! It's on sale today.

(5) You and your friend are planning what to do on the weekend.

A: 주말에 뭐 할까요? What should we do this weekend?

B: 음, 영화 ______________________. Well, I want to watch a movie.

A: 와, 좋아요. 영화관에 갈까요? Sounds good! Shall we go to the movies?

(6) You're at a café, deciding what to drink.

A: 우리 뭐 마실까요? What should we drink?

B: 저는 아메리카노 ______________________. I want to drink an Americano.

A: 저도 아메리카노 마실래요. I'll have an Americano too.

(7) You're talking with your friend about where you want to travel.

A: 어느 나라 여행하고 싶어요? Which country do you want to travel to?

B: 저는 호주를 ______________________. I want to travel to Australia.

UNIT 24

V-고 있어요

am/are/is doing ~

Video 30

When you are talking about what you are doing right now, you use **-고 있어요**. It's similar to "I am doing ~" in English. You can also use it to talk about things you've been doing these days, like work, hobbies, or ongoing activities. Unlike "be ~ing" in English, **-고 있어요** is not used for future actions.

CRACKING THE PATTERN CODE

The pattern -고 있어요 is also very simple to use. Just attach -고 있어요 to the verb stem!

먹다 → 먹**고 있어요**　　쓰다 → 쓰**고 있어요**　　만들다 → 만들**고 있어요**

The basic form of -고 있어요 is -고 있다. To make different tenses, you change the ending:

-고 있어요 am/are doing (*present*)

-고 있었어요 was doing (*past*)

-고 있을 거예요 will be doing (*future guess*)

In honorific forms, use -고 계세요 instead of -고 있어요.

A: 알렉스 씨는 지금 뭐 해요? What is Alex doing now?

B: (알렉스 씨는) 운동하고 있어요. He's working out.

A: 할머니는 지금 뭐 하세요? What is your grandmother doing now?

B: (할머니는) 운동하고 계세요. She's working out. (*honorific*)

유튜브 Youtube • 할머니 grandmother

CORE SENTENCES

MP3 58

기다리다	친구를	**기다리**	고 있어요.	I am waiting for my friend.
가다	지금 집에	**가**	고 있어요.	I am going home now.
듣다	요즘 클래식을	**듣**	고 있어요.	I am listening to classical music these days.
일하다	은행에서	**일하**	고 있어요.	I am working at a bank.
가르치다	영어를	**가르치**	고 있어요.	I am teaching English.
도와드리다	엄마를	**도와드리**	고 있어요.	I am helping my mom. *(honorific)*
찾다	화장실을	**찾**	고 있어요.	I am looking for the bathroom.
쉬다	선생님은	**쉬**	고 계세요.	The teacher is taking a rest. (*honorific*)
요리하다	아빠는	**요리하**	고 계세요.	Dad is cooking. (*honorific*)
주무시다	할머니는	**주무시**	고 계세요.	My grandmother is sleeping. (*honorific*)

Essential Practices

MP3 59

1. Change each verb into the -고 있어요 form and say it out loud.

기다리다 → 기다리고 있어요 to wait	가다 → ________ to go	자다 → ________ to sleep
일하다 → ________ to work	가르치다 → ________ to teach	요리하다 → ________ to cook
식사하다 → ________ to have a meal	찾다 → ________ to find, to look for	듣다 → ________ to listen
배우다 → ________ to learn	도와드리다 → ________ to help	팔다 → ________ to sell

2. Complete each sentence using -고 있어요 or -고 계세요 to match the English meaning. Use the hint words in parentheses.

(1) I am teaching English.
(영어, 가르치다)
= 저는 영어(를) 가르치고 있어요.

(2) Dad is making breakfast now.
(아침, 만들다)
= 아빠는 지금 아침(을) 만들고 계세요.
(honorific)

(3) I'm looking for the bus station.
(찾다, 버스 정류장)
= ________ ________.

(4) I'm studying Korean these days.
(한국어, 공부하다)
= 요즘 ________ ________.

(5) I am writing in my diary every day.
(일기, 쓰다)
= 매일 ________ ________.

(6) Mom is reading the newspaper now.
(신문, 읽다)
= 엄마는 지금 ________ ________.
(honorific)

3. **Read the situations and complete each conversation using the -고 있어요 pattern. Use each word in the box only once.**

~~가다~~	가르치다	찾다	식사하다	듣다

(1) You are late to a get-together with friends. One of them calls to ask where you are.

A: 지금 어디예요? 모두 기다리고 있어요. Where are you now? Everyone's waiting.

B: 미안해요. 지금 __가고 있어요__. Sorry. I'm on my way.

(2) You meet someone new and ask about their job.

A: 무슨 일 하세요? What do you do?

B: 저는 영어를 ____________________. 무슨 일 하세요? I teach English. What do you do?

A: 저는 학생이에요. I'm a student.

(3) You are in a clothing store, looking for a shirt.

A: 뭐 찾으세요? 도와드릴까요? What are you looking for? Can I help you?

B: 아, 셔츠를 ____________________. Oh, I'm looking for a shirt.

A: 셔츠는 저쪽에 있어요. The shirts are over there.

B: 감사합니다. Thank you.

(4) You ask your coworker what the boss is doing right now.

A: 지수 씨, 사장님 지금 뭐 하고 계세요? Jisoo, what is the boss doing now?

B: ____________________. She is having a meal. (*honorific*)

(5) You're texting with a friend and talking about what you're doing now.

A: 지금 뭐 해요? What are you doing now?

B: 음악 ____________________. I'm listening to music.

A: 오, 무슨 음악 들어요? Oh, what kind of music are you listening to?

UNIT 25

A-(으)ㄴ데요, V-는데요

~, and/but...

Video 31

The pattern -(으)ㄴ/는데요 is often used to start a conversation or invite a response. It makes your speech sound softer and more natural.

For example, if you say **지하철역을 찾는데요** (I am looking for a subway station...), the listener understands you probably need help. This sounds more polite than directly asking **지하철역이 어디에 있어요?** (Where is the subway station?).

You can also use it to bring up a topic, like **어제 드라마를 봤는데요** (I watched a drama yesterday...), which invites the listener to respond or ask more.

Depending on the situation, **-(으)ㄴ/는데요** can imply "and...", "but...", or simply hint that more is coming. In other words, it's a soft way to connect your thoughts or invite the listener into the conversation.

CRACKING THE PATTERN CODE

To use the pattern A-(으)ㄴ데요 / V-는데요, you need to look at the type of word you are using.

Use -(으)ㄴ데요 only in two cases—**adjectives (present)** and -고 싶어요 (-고 싶다) phrase. For almost everything else, just use -는데요.

Adjective (present) -고 싶다	+	-(으)ㄴ데요
Verb (present) 있다 / 없다 Past tense -았/었-	+	-는데요

1 Adjective (present) + -(으)ㄴ데요: -은데요 or -ㄴ데요

작다 → 작은데요
└ 받침 O

크다 → 큰데요
└ 받침 X

달다 → 단데요
└ ends in ㄹ, so drop ㄹ

This pattern is often used with -고 싶다 (I want to...), which we treat like an adjective.

사고 싶다 → 사고 싶은데요
└ 받침 O

먹고 싶다 → 먹고 싶은데요
└ 받침 O

2 Verb (present) + -는데요

Use -는데요 with all verbs in the present tense.

공부하다 → 공부하는데요

먹다 → 먹는데요

살다 → 사는데요
└ ends in ㄹ, so drop ㄹ

3 있다 / 없다 + -는데요

Whether it's used like an adjective or a verb, 있다 / 없다 always takes -는데요.

맛있다 → 맛있는데요

재미없다 → 재미없는데요

찾고 있다 → 찾고 있는데요

할 수 없다 → 할 수 없는데요

4 Past tense: A/V-았/었는데요

For both verbs and adjectives in the past tense, use -았/었는데요.

가다 → 갔어요 *(past)* → 갔는데요

먹다 → 먹었어요 *(past)* → 먹었는데요

좋다 → 좋았어요 *(past)* → 좋았는데요

작다 → 작았어요 *(past)* → 작았는데요

Tip!

To change N이에요/예요 sentences, use N인데요, regardless of the final consonant.
In the past tense, use -이었는데요 (after a consonant) or -였는데요 (after a vowel).

지하철역 [지하철력] subway station • 찾다 to find, to look for • 이쪽으로 this way • 작다 to be small • 크다 to be big • 살다 to live • 할 수 없다[할 쑤 업따] can't do

CORE SENTENCES

MP3 60

[Adjective, -고 싶다] + -(으)ㄴ데요

아프다	머리가 좀	아픈데요.	My head hurts a bit, ... (And could you give me some medicine?)
더럽다*	방이 좀	더러운데요.	The room is a bit dirty, ... (Can you clean it? / Can I get another room?)
필요하다	도움이 좀	필요한데요.	I need help, ... (Could you help me?)
쓰고 싶다	화장실을	쓰고 싶은데요.	I'd like to use the restroom, ... (And where is it? / May I use it?)
사고 싶다	이거	사고 싶은데요.	I want to buy this, ... (How much is it? / Can I buy this?)

[Verb, 있다/없다, past tense] + -는데요

없다	방에 수건이	없는데요.	There are no towels in the room, ... (Could you bring me some towels?)
찾고 있다	서울역을	찾고 있는데요.	I'm looking for Seoul Station, ... (Can you tell me where it is?)
샀어요	어제 이걸	샀는데요.	I bought this yesterday, ... (I have a question/problem about it.)
예약했어요	'John Smith'로	예약했는데요.	I made a reservation under "John Smith," ... (I'm here to check in / to claim the reservation.)
시켰어요	아까 라면을	시켰는데요.	I ordered ramyeon earlier, ... (But it hasn't come yet / this isn't what I ordered.)

* irregular form (ㅂ → 우)

Tip!

The word **필요하다** means "to need," but it's actually an adjective in Korean. So in dictionaries, it may be translated as "to be necessary." In real conversations, you can say **N이/가 필요해요** to mean "I need (something)."

Essential Practices

MP3 61

1. Change each word into the -(으)ㄴ/는데요 form and say it out loud. Decide which one to use based on the type of word.

아프다 → 아픈데요 to be sick, to hurt	작다 → ______ to be small	달다 → ______ to be sweet
필요하다 → ______ to need, to be necessary	피곤하다 → ______ to be tired	사고 싶다 → ______ to want to buy
더럽다* → ______ to be dirty (adjective)	덥다* → ______ to be hot (adjective)	굽다 → ______ to bake/grill (verb)
맛있다 → ______ to be delicious	재미있다 → ______ to be fun	없다 → ______ not to be, not to have
할 수 있다 → ______ can do something	시켰어요 → ______ I ordered	예약했어요 → ______ I made a reservation

2. Change the sentence into the -(으)ㄴ/는데요 form.

(1) 방이 더러워요. → 방이 더러운데요. The room is a bit dirty, ...

(2) 수건이 없어요. → ______. There are no towels, ...

(3) 백화점을 찾고 있어요. → ______. I'm looking for the department store, ...

(4) 이거 사고 싶어요. → ______. I want to buy this, ...

(5) 배가 아파요. → ______. My stomach hurts, ...

(6) 현금이 없어요. → ______. I don't have cash, ...

3. Read the situation and make a sentence to begin the conversation using -(으)ㄴ/는데요. Use each word in the box only once.

~~사고 싶다~~	찾고 있다	예약했어요	쓰고 싶다	시켰어요

(1) You want to buy a bag in a store and ask for a price.

A: 이 가방 사고 싶은데요. 얼마예요? I'd like to buy this bag. How much is it?

B: 3만원이에요. It's 30,000 won.

(2) You are in a café and want to ask if you can use the restroom.

A: 화장실을 좀 ________________________. I'd like to use the restroom.

B: 네, 저쪽에 있어요. Okay, it's over there.

(3) You can't find the bus stop and want to ask someone nearby for directions.

A: 저, 버스 정류장을 ________________________. Excuse me, I'm looking for the bus stop.

B: 아, 저쪽으로 가세요. Oh, go that way.

(4) You're at the hotel front desk and want to check in with your name.

A: 안녕하세요. 'Alex Kim'으로 ________________________. Hello. I have a reservation under "Alex Kim."

B: 네, 잠시만 기다려 주십시오. Sure, just a moment, please.

(5) You ordered an iced Americano at a café, but they gave you a hot one.

A: 저는 아이스 아메리카노를 ________________________. I ordered an iced Americano...
바꿔 주실 수 있어요? Could you change it, please?

B: 죄송합니다. 바로 다시 드릴게요! Sorry. I'll get you a new one right away!

EXPLORE FURTHER

Other Ways to Use -(으)ㄴ/는데요

In this unit, we focused on using **-(으)ㄴ/는데요** to start a conversation or invite a response. But you'll also hear this pattern used in other ways.

1 To show surprise or a personal reaction

When you're pleasantly surprised or impressed by something, you can use **-(으)ㄴ/는데요**. It's similar to **-네요** in meaning. The tone usually rises slightly at the end, showing surprise or interest.

A: **이 케이크 어때요? 제가 만들었어요!** How's this cake? I made it!

B: **와, 맛있는데요!** Wow, it's really good!

2 To politely give a different opinion or say no

You can also use **-(으)ㄴ/는데요** to respond politely when you disagree or can't accept a suggestion. It's like saying "Well... actually..." or "I'm afraid..." in English. The tone often falls at the end, showing hesitation or soft refusal.

A: **내일 같이 피크닉 갈까요?** Shall we go on a picnic together tomorrow?

B: 어떡하죠? **내일은 약속이 있는데요...**
Oh no... I actually have plans tomorrow... (so I think I can't make it tomorrow.)

UNIT 26

Sentence Power-Ups: Extra Expressions 문장을 더 풍부하게 : 추가 표현

You've done a great job practicing many different patterns and building sentences. Now it's time for a final level-up! Check out the extra words and markers to make your Korean even more expressive. Follow the gray words and write them out as you go to help remember their meanings.

TIME EXPRESSIONS

MP3 62

1 Year, Month, Week Words

작년 last year	올해 this year	내년 next year
지난달 last month	이번 달 this month	다음 달 next month
지난주 last week	이번 주 this week	다음 주 next week

These words usually take the time marker 에, except for 올해 (this year). 올해 is used without the marker.

작년에 한국에 갔어요. (○)   올해에 한국에 가요. (×)   올해 한국에 가요. (○)

2 Day Words

그저께	어제	오늘	내일	모레
the day before yesterday	yesterday	today	tomorrow	the day after tomorrow

Day words are adverbs, so they are used without the time marker **에**.

어제에 영화를 봤어요. (×) **어제 영화를 봤어요. (○)**

3 Useful Time Adverbs

지난번에	아까	지금	이따가	나중에
last time	a little while ago	now	later (in a while)	later (in the future)

아까 refers to something that happened earlier today, usually within the last few hours. **지난번에** covers a broader, less specific past.

이따가 means after a little time has passed, usually later today (soon). In spoken Korean, **이따가** is often shortened to **이따**. **나중에** means later in a more general sense, including days in the future.

MARKERS FOR TIME, PLACE, AND MORE

MP3 63

1 Time and Place

Markers	Examples	
N에 at time	A: 언제 자요? B: 10시**에** 자요.	A: When do you go to bed? B: I go to bed at 10.
N에 ① (go) to place ② (exist) at place	① A: 어디 가요? B: 학교**에** 가요. ② A: 지금 어디 있어요? B: 학교**에** 있어요.	① A: Where are you going? B: I'm going to school. ② A: Where are you now? B: I'm at school.
N에서 (doing something) at place	A: 어디**에서** 공부해요? B: 학교**에서** 공부해요.	A: Where do you study? B: I study at school.

N(으)로 to direction/somewhere *받침 O+ 으로 / 받침 X, ㄹ + 로	이쪽으로 가세요.	Go this way, please.
~부터 ...까지 from time to time	9시부터 5시까지 일해요.	I work from 9 to 5.
~에서 ...까지 from place to place	집에서 학교까지 멀어요?	Is it far from home to school?

Use **N에서** when an action happens at a place. Use **N에** with **있어요** or **없어요** to show where something exists or doesn't exist.

2 Means and Roles

Markers	Examples	
N(으)로 ① by means ② with a tool or method ③ as a role or identity *받침 O+ 으로 / 받침 X, ㄹ + 로	① A: 학교에 어떻게 가요? B: 지하철로 가요.	A: How do you go to school? B: I go by subway.
	② A: 연필로 써도 돼요? B: 펜으로 쓰세요.	A: Can I write with a pencil? B: Write with a pen, please.
	③ A: 병원에서 무슨 일을 해요? B: 의사로 일해요.	A: What do you do in the hospital? B: I work as a doctor.

PLACE AND DIRECTION WORDS

MP3 64

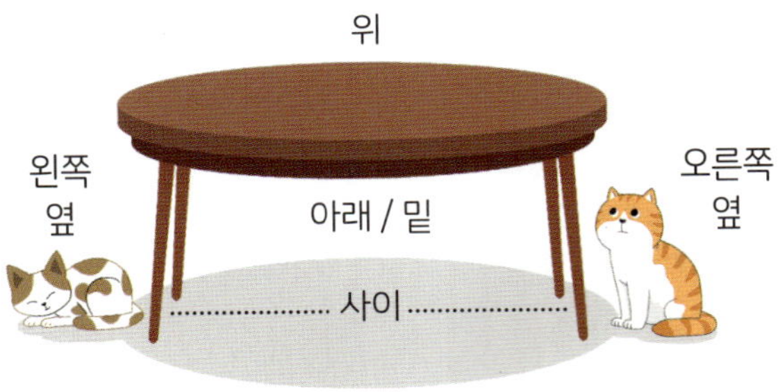

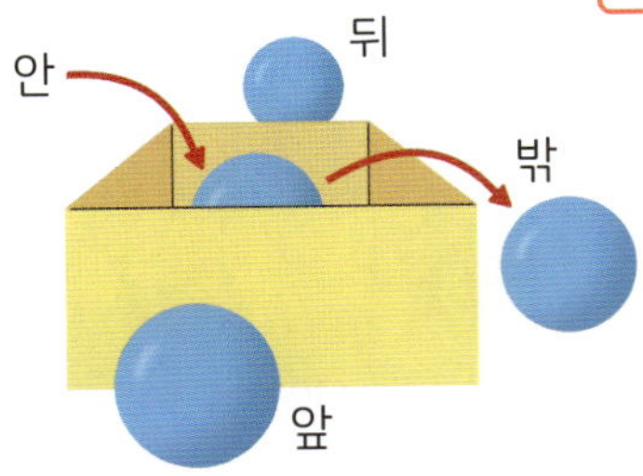

Words	Examples	
위 on, above	책상 **위**에 책이 있어요.	There is a book on the desk.
아래 / 밑 under, below	책상 **밑**에 책이 있어요. 책상 **아래**에 책이 있어요.	There is a book under the desk.
옆 beside, next to	책상 **옆**에 고양이가 있어요.	There is a cat beside the desk.
사이 between	고양이들 **사이**에 책상이 있어요.	There is a desk between the cats.
왼쪽 left	책상 **왼쪽**에 고양이가 있어요.	There is a cat to the left of the desk.
오른쪽 right	책상 **오른쪽**에 고양이가 있어요.	There is a cat to the right of the desk.
앞 front	상자 **앞**에 공이 있어요.	There is a ball in front of the box.
뒤 behind	상자 **뒤**에 공이 있어요.	There is a ball behind the box.
안 in, inside	상자 **안**에 공이 있어요.	There is a ball in the box.
밖 out, outside	상자 **밖**에 공이 있어요.	There is a ball outside the box.

MARKERS FOR CONNECTING PEOPLE, THINGS, AND ACTIONS

MP3 65

1 Connecting and Listing: with, and

Markers	Examples	
N하고 with N (informal)	친구**하고** 학교에 가요.	I go to school with my friend.
N와/과 with N (formal) *받침 O + 과 / 받침 X + 와	친구**와** 학교에 갑니다.	I go to school with my friend.
N하고 N N and N (informal)	물**하고** 커피 주세요.	Water and coffee, please.
N와/과 N N and N (formal)	과일**과** 빵을 샀습니다.	I bought some fruit and bread.

N와/과 sounds more formal than **N하고**. In casual speech, **N(이)랑** is also commonly used. When listing several things, you can repeat the particle after each noun, like this: **사과하고 라면하고 커피하고 피자하고...**

2 Possession and Addition: of, also

Markers	Examples	
N의 N N of N (possessive)	친구**의** 핸드폰	My friend's phone
N도 also N, too, either	A: 저는 차를 좋아해요. 커피**도** 좋아해요. B: 오, 저**도** 커피 좋아해요.	A: I like tea. I also like coffee. B: Oh, I like coffee, too.

The possessive marker **의** can be pronounced [에] in speech: **친구의** [친구의 or 친구에]. The possessive marker **의** is often omitted: **친구 핸드폰**.

The marker **도** replaces topic marker **은/는**, subject marker **이/가**, or object marker **을/를**. For other markers, just add **도** after them, like in **와도/과도**, **에게도**, **한테도**, and so on.

3 Giving and Receiving: to, from

Markers	Examples	
N에게 to someone (formal, informal)	친구**에게** 선물을 줬어요.	I gave a present to my friend.
N한테 to someone (casual, informal)	친구**한테** 선물을 줬어요.	I gave a present to my friend.
N에게(서) from someone (formal, informal)	친구**에게(서)** 선물을 받았어요.	I got a present from my friend.
N한테(서) from someone (casual, informal)	친구**한테(서)** 선물을 받았어요.	I got a present from my friend.

에게서/한테서 (from someone) is often used as 에게/한테. So look at the verb and the context carefully.

4 Honorific Equivalents for Markers

When using honorifics, some markers change if the subject or the person you're referring to is someone you should respect. However, what matters most is the verb ending. Using polite forms like -(으)세요 is usually enough to show respect.

Basic Form	Honorific Form
이/가	께서
은/는	께서는
을/를	을/를 (no change)
도	께서도
에게 / 한테	께
에게(서) / 한테(서)	

ADVERBS FOR CONNECTIONS AND EMPHASIS

MP3 66

1 Frequency Adverbs

Words	Examples	
항상 / 늘 / 언제나 always	**항상** 커피를 마셔요.	I always drink coffee.
자주 often	음악을 **자주** 들어요.	I often listen to music.
가끔 sometimes	**가끔** 운동해요.	I exercise sometimes.
별로 안 not much	초콜릿을 **별로 안** 먹어요.	I don't really eat chocolate.
거의 안 rarely	**거의 안** 자요.	I rarely sleep.
전혀 안 not at all	술을 **전혀 안** 마셔요.	I don't drink alcohol at all.

2 Adverbs for Emphasis

Words	Examples	
정말 really	이 영화 **정말** 재미있어요.	This movie is really fun.
제일 the most	김밥이 **제일** 좋아요.	I like gimbap the most.
많이 a lot	한국 음식을 **많이** 먹어요.	I eat Korean food a lot.
아주 very	**아주** 맛있어요!	It's very delicious!
너무 too much	**너무** 추워요.	It's too cold.

너무 literally means "too much," but in daily speech, it's also used in a positive way: **너무 예뻐요! 너무 좋아요!**

3 Connective Adverbs

Words	Examples
그리고 and	책을 읽어요. **그리고** 음악을 들어요. I read a book. And I listen to music.
그래서 that's why	날씨가 추워요. **그래서** 집에 있을 거예요. It's cold. That's why I'm going to stay home.
그러니까 so	바쁘지요? **그러니까** 나중에 만나요. You're busy, right? So let's meet later.
그렇지만 / 하지만 [그러치만] but	떡볶이가 맛있어요. **그렇지만** 매워요. Tteokbokki is delicious. But it's spicy.
그런데 ① but ② by the way	① 배가 고팠어요. **그런데** 먹을 것이 없었어요. I was hungry. But I had nothing to eat. ② 날씨가 좋네요! **그런데** 내일 시간 있어요? What a great day! By the way, are you free tomorrow?
그래도 but still, even so	피곤해요. **그래도** 운동해요. I'm tired. But still, I exercise.
그러면 then, if so	한국어를 많이 연습하세요. **그러면** 잘할 수 있어요. Practice Korean a lot. If you do, you'll get good at it.

After **그래서** comes a result. After **그러니까** comes a suggestion or command. Use **그렇지만** or **하지만** for clear, logical contrast. Use **그런데** to connect ideas naturally or to change the topic.

4 Connective Adverbs and Related Grammar Endings

The connective adverbs you just learned are also related to grammar endings used to connect two or more clauses.

Adverbs	Grammar Endings	Examples
그리고 and	-고	책을 읽어요. 그리고 음악을 들어요. ➡ 책을 읽고 음악을 들어요.
그래서 that's why	-아/어서	날씨가 추워요. 그래서 집에 있어요. ➡ 날씨가 추워서 집에 있을 거예요.
그러니까 so	-(으)니까	바쁘지요? 그러니까 나중에 만나요. ➡ 바쁘니까 나중에 만나요.
그렇지만 / 하지만 but	-지만	떡볶이가 맛있어요. 그렇지만 매워요. ➡ 떡볶이가 맛있지만 매워요.
그런데 but	-(으)ㄴ데/는데	배가 고팠어요. 그런데 먹을 것이 없었어요. ➡ 배가 고팠는데 먹을 것이 없었어요.
그래도 but still, even so	-아/어도	피곤해요. 그래도 운동해요. ➡ 피곤해도 운동해요.
그러면 then, if so	-(으)면	한국어를 많이 연습하세요. 그러면 잘할 수 있어요. ➡ 한국어를 많이 연습하면 잘할 수 있어요.

PART 3

Let's Talk! In Real Situations

Great job learning the basics of Korean—from Hangeul to key grammar patterns. Now let's put it all into practice with real-life conversations. In this part, you'll practice simple and practical dialogues based on everyday situations.

The first unit introduces useful conversation openers and reactions. After that, each unit presents three scenario-based dialogues that match the unit's theme. Start by reading the situation at the top of each dialogue to understand the context.

Use the audio tracks to listen, repeat, and role-play each conversation out loud. For best results, we recommend practicing each dialogue at least three times. Use the *Practice Tracker* beside the dialogue to check off each round and track your progress.

In the *Structure Review* section, you'll practice each line more closely by tracing sentences and completing guided exercises to make the language your own. You can start with the *Structure Review* to better understand the sentence patterns before reading the dialogue out loud, or do the review after speaking. Either way works.

Remember, you don't need to speak perfectly. The goal is to speak regularly and with confidence. Let's talk!

UNIT 1

Conversation Openers & Reactions 대화 시작하기 & 반응하기

Before starting full conversations, let's learn simple phrases to start talking and react naturally. These expressions will help you sound friendlier and fluent in daily situations. Practice saying them out loud —you'll use them all the time!

STARTING A CONVERSATION

MP3 67

Excuse me.

저, / 저기요. / 실례합니다.

저, 저기요, and 실례합니다 are polite ways to get someone's attention, such as when asking for directions or speaking to a stranger. They're commonly used as interjections in these situations. 안녕하세요 can also be used like "excuse me" in public places. 실례합니다 is very formal and rarely used in daily conversation, so people usually prefer 저 or 저기요. In cafés and restaurants, customers often call staff by saying 여기요! (Over here!), especially from their seat.

Sorry, but... / Excuse me, but...

죄송한데... / 실례지만...

죄송한데... and 실례지만... are also used to politely begin a question or request, especially when speaking to someone you don't know well. Similar to 실례합니다, 실례지만 is very formal and rarely used in everyday Korean. 죄송한데... is polite enough for most everyday situations.

EXPRESSING REACTIONS & EMOTIONS

MP3 68

Well... / Hmm...	Oh!	Wow!
음... / 흠...	**아!**	**와!**

These are interjections that help express hesitation, realization, or surprise. You can use them freely depending on how you feel in the moment—they're not tied to specific situations.

Really?

정말요? / 진짜요?

Is that so?

그래요?

I see.

그렇군요.

[그러쿠뇨]

정말요?/진짜요? and 그래요? aren't necessarily real questions. They're more about showing that you're listening and engaged. These expressions show interest and help keep the conversation flowing. 그렇군요 is used when you realize or accept new information, kind of like saying "Oh, I see." It shows that you're listening and processing what was said.

Oh no, / Oh my, / Oh dear,

아이고,

아이고 is a versatile exclamation used in both positive and negative situations. It often shows sympathy, like when someone is sick, but it can also express delight or surprise—like when you're happy to see a friend or reacting to something good. It's also used in self-talk, just like "Oh my" or "Oh dear" in English.

AGREEING & RESPONDING

MP3 69

That's right.

맞아요.

Of course!

그럼요!

맞아요 and 그럼요! are commonly used to politely answer confirmation questions. They're also used to agree with someone or to show you understand.

To politely say no or disagree, you can use 아니요 (No), which you've already learned. To politely correct someone or respond to a compliment, use 아니에요 (Not at all).

Sounds good.

좋아요.

좋아요 is used when you agree to a suggestion or say yes to a plan.

Me too.

저도요.

저도요 is used when you share the same opinion, feeling, or experience.

USEFUL PHRASES IN PUBLIC PLACES

MP3 70

Please ring me up. / I'd like to pay.

계산해 주세요. / 계산할게요.

[계산할께요]

Use these when you're ready to pay. **계산할게요** is slightly more casual than **계산해 주세요**, but both are polite and common.

Here you are.

여기 있어요.

여기 있어요 is used when you hand something to someone, like cash, a card, or your ID. You can also say **여기요**—in this case, it means "Here you are," not "Over here." You'll also hear these expressions from staff when they hand something to you. In more formal settings, such as at hotel front desks, staff may say **여기 있습니다**, which is a formal speech style.

Please wait a moment.

잠시만/잠깐만 기다려 주세요.

Just a moment.

잠시만요.

잠시만/잠깐만 기다려 주세요 and **잠시만요** are used when asking someone to wait briefly—such as in a store, a restaurant, or at a busy counter.

☑ Self-Check

1. **Match the English meanings with the correct Korean expressions.**

(1) 실례합니다. •	• ① I see.
(2) 계산해 주세요. •	• ② Excuse me.
(3) 그렇군요. •	• ③ Here you are.
(4) 여기 있어요. •	• ④ Just a moment.
(5) 잠시만요. •	• ⑤ Me too.
(6) 저도요. •	• ⑥ Please ring me up.

2. **Choose the best expression for each situation.**

여기 있어요　　그럼요　　저기요　　잠시만요　　좋아요　　아이고　　정말요

(1) You want to ask a stranger for directions on the street.

→ ____________, 죄송한데 지하철역이 어디예요?

(2) Your friend just told you she's going on a trip to Korea.

→ 와, ____________? 저도 가고 싶어요!

(3) A cashier finishes ringing up your items. You hand over your credit card.

→ ________________.

(4) On a train, someone asks if they can sit in the empty seat next to you. You're happy to say yes.

→ ____________! 여기 앉으세요.

(5) You're still looking at the menu when the server comes to take your order. You need a bit more time.

→ 아, ____________. 메뉴 좀 더 볼게요.

(6) Your friend suggests going to a Korean restaurant for lunch. You think it's a great idea.

→ 와, ____________! 같이 가요!

(7) Your friend says they're sick and feeling tired. You want to show concern and tell them to rest.

→ ____________, 푹 쉬세요.

[Answer Key] **1.** (1) ② (2) ⑥ (3) ① (4) ③ (5) ④ (6) ⑤
2. (1) 저기요 (2) 정말요 (3) 여기 있어요 (4) 그럼요 (5) 잠시만요 (6) 좋아요 (7) 아이고

WRITING CONVERSATION OPENERS & REACTIONS

Let's read each expression out loud, then try writing it yourself.

1 Starting a Conversation

저, Excuse me,	저,	
저기요. Excuse me.	저기요.	
실례합니다. Excuse me.	실례합니다.	
죄송한데... Sorry, but...	죄송한데...	
실례지만... Excuse me, but...	실례지만...	

2 Expressing Reactions & Emotions

음... Well...	음...	
흠... Hmm...	흠...	
아! Oh!	아!	
와! Wow!	와!	
정말요? Really?	정말요?	
진짜요? Really?	진짜요?	

그래요? Is that so?	그래요?	
그렇군요. I see.	그렇군요.	
아이고, Oh no, / Oh my, / Oh dear,	아이고,	

3 Agreeing & Responding

맞아요. That's right.	맞아요.	
그럼요! Of course!	그럼요!	
좋아요. Sounds good.	좋아요.	
저도요. Me too.	저도요.	

4 Useful Phrases in Public Places

계산해 주세요. Please ring me up.	계산해 주세요.	
계산할게요. I'd like to pay.	계산할게요.	
여기 있어요. Here you go.	여기 있어요.	
잠시만 기다려 주세요. Please wait a moment.	잠시만 기다려 주세요.	
잠깐만 기다려 주세요. Please wait a moment.	잠깐만 기다려 주세요.	
잠시만요. Just a moment.	잠시만요.	

UNIT 2

Greeting Others and Introducing Yourself 인사와 소개

Let's practice how to greet others at moments of **인사** (greeting) and talk about yourself through **소개** (introducing yourself). Imagine you're in class, on a trip, or meeting someone new. Try changing your name or nationality to make it your own!

Key Patterns

- **N이에요/예요** PART II - UNIT 5
- **A/V-아/어요** PART II - UNIT 10
- **A/V았/었어요** PART II - UNIT 14
- **A/V-네요** PART II - UNIT 16
- **V-고 있어요** PART II - UNIT 24

SCENARIO 1

Imagine you're in your Korean class, introducing yourself to your classmates. This is your chance to demonstrate the Korean you've been working so hard on!

CONVERSATION

MP3 71

You 안녕하세요? 저는 리사예요.
Hello. I am Lisa.

저는 영국에서 왔어요.
I came from the UK.

저는 선생님이에요. 학교에서 영어를 가르쳐요.
I'm a teacher. I teach English at school.

만나서 반갑습니다.
Nice to meet you.

Others 반가워요!
Nice to meet you!

Practice Tracker

☐ ☐ ☐

Words & Phrases

학교 school

영어 English (language)

가르쳐요
↳ 가르치다 to teach

Tip!

영국에서 왔어요 means "I am from the UK = I came from the UK," which is the same as **영국 사람이에요**. Remember that you always need to use **왔어요** (past tense of **오다**), same as when you introduce yourself in English.

STRUCTURE REVIEW

1 Trace over the gray text to get familiar with each sentence. As you write, say the sentences out loud to help with pronunciation and fluency.

You 안녕하세요? 저는 리사예요.

저는 영국에서 왔어요.

저는 선생님이에요.

학교에서 영어를 가르쳐요.

만나서 반갑습니다.

Others 반가워요!

2 Complete the dialogue using the hint words with the appropriate patterns and particles.

You 안녕하세요? ______________________.
(저, 리사)

저는 영국에서 ______________________.
(오다)

저는 ______________________.
(선생님)

학교에서 영어를 ______________________.
(가르치다)

만나서 ______________________.
(반갑다)

Others 반가워요!

SCENARIO 2

You're on a flight to Seoul and having a small chat with the person next to you. It's a great opportunity to practice the Korean you already know!

CONVERSATION

MP3 72

A 저, 혹시 한국 사람이세요?
Excuse me, but are you Korean by any chance?

B 네, 맞아요.
Yes, I am.

A 반가워요! 저는 니코예요. 이탈리아 사람이에요.
Nice to meet you! I'm Nico. I'm Italian.

B 반갑습니다. 저는 지수예요. 한국어 잘하시네요!
Nice to meet you. I'm Jisu. Your Korean is really good!

A 감사합니다. 열심히 공부하고 있어요.
Thank you. I've been studying hard.
그럼 편안한 여행 되세요!
Well then, I hope you have a comfortable trip!

B 네, 감사해요! 니코 씨도요!
Yes, thank you! You too, Nico!

Practice Tracker

☐ ☐ ☐

Words & Phrases

혹시 by any chance

이탈리아 사람 Italian (person)

잘하시네요!
└, 잘하다 to be good at sth

열심히 [열씸히] hard

공부하고 있어요
└, 공부하다 to study

그럼 well then

편안한 여행 되세요!
Have a comfortable trip!
└, 편안하다 to be comfortable
└, 여행 trip, travel

Tip!

In the phrase **편안한 여행 되세요**!, **편안한** (comfortable) is used because the expression often refers to situations such as flights, similar to how English speakers say "Have a comfortable flight." You can use [**modifier** + **situation/event**] + **되세요** to express good wishes for an event or situation like: **즐거운 크리스마스 되세요**! (Merry Christmas!) or **좋은 하루 되세요**! (Have a good day!).

STRUCTURE REVIEW

1 Trace over the gray text to get familiar with each sentence. As you write, say the sentences out loud to help with pronunciation and fluency.

A 저, 혹시 ___한국 사람이세요___?

B 네, 맞아요.

A 반가워요! ___저는 니코예요___.
___이탈리아 사람이에요___.

B 반갑습니다. ___저는 지수예요___.
___한국어 잘하시네요___!

A 감사합니다. ___열심히 공부하고 있어요___.
그럼 ___편안한 여행 되세요___!

B 네, 감사해요! 니코 씨도요!

2 Complete the dialogue using the hint words with the appropriate patterns and particles.

A 저, 혹시 ______________________? (한국 사람)

B 네, 맞아요.

A 반가워요! ______________________ (저, 니코). ______________________ (이탈리아 사람).

B 반갑습니다. 저는 지수예요. 한국어 잘하시네요!

A 감사합니다. 열심히 ______________________ (공부하다).
그럼 편안한 여행 되세요!

B 네, 감사해요! 니코 씨도요!

SCENARIO 3

You don't have to be in a Korean class or travel to Korea to use Korean in real life. You might meet a Korean traveler in your own country, and this could be the perfect chance to start a conversation! Imagine you just met a Korean visitor—how would you introduce yourself?

CONVERSATION

MP3 73

A 안녕하세요. 혹시 한국 분이세요?
Hello. Are you Korean by any chance?

B 네. 한국 사람이에요. 와, 한국어 잘하시네요!
Yes, I'm Korean. Wow, your Korean is really good!

A 감사합니다. 저는 한국어를 배우고 있어요.
Thank you. I'm learning Korean.

그래서 한국어로 인사해 봤어요.
So I tried greeting you in Korean.

여행 중이세요?
Are you traveling?

B 네. 맞아요.
Yes, I am.

A 그렇군요. 즐거운 여행 되세요!
I see. Have a pleasant trip!

B 네, 감사합니다!
Yes, thank you!

Practice Tracker

☐ ☐ ☐

Words & Phrases

분 person (honorific form of 사람)

인사해 봤어요
└ 인사해 보다 to try greeting

즐거운 여행 되세요! Have a nice trip!
└ 즐겁다 to be pleasant

Tip!

In the phrase **여행 중이세요?**, notice the [Noun] + 중 pattern. This structure is used to indicate that someone is in the middle of doing something or that a process is currently happening. You can see this in phrases like **회의 중이에요**. (I am in a meeting.), **지금 통화 중이에요**. (I am on a call right now.), and **공사 중입니다**. (Construction is in progress.).

STRUCTURE REVIEW

1 Trace over the gray text to get familiar with each sentence. As you write, say the sentences out loud to help with pronunciation and fluency.

A 안녕하세요. 혹시 한국 분이세요?

B 네. 한국 사람이에요. 와, 한국어 잘하시네요!

A 감사합니다. 저는 한국어를 배우고 있어요.

그래서 한국어로 인사해 봤어요.

여행 중이세요?

B 네. 맞아요.

A 그렇군요. 즐거운 여행 되세요!

B 네, 감사합니다!

2 Complete the dialogue using the hint words with the appropriate patterns and particles.

A 안녕하세요. 혹시 ______________________?
(한국 분)

B 네. 한국 사람이에요. 와, 한국어 잘하시네요!

A 감사합니다. 저는 한국어를 ______________________.
(배우다)

그래서 한국어로 ______________________.
(인사해 보다)

______________________?
(여행 중)

B 네. 맞아요.

A 그렇군요. ______________________!
(즐거운 여행, 되다)

B 네, 감사합니다!

UNIT 3

Talking about Daily Life

일상 이야기하기

Talking about your **일상** (daily life) is a great way to connect with Korean friends. Let's practice talking about your everyday life, from when you study to what you do on weekends. These small moments make great conversations!

Key Patterns

- **N이에요/예요** PART II - UNIT 5
- **A/V-지요?** PART II - UNIT 15
- **안 A/V, 못 V** PART II - UNIT 11
- **V-고 있어요** PART II - UNIT 24
- **A/V-았/었어요** PART II - UNIT 14
- **V-(으)ㄹ 거예요** PART II - UNIT 21

SCENARIO 1

You're meeting your Korean language exchange partner for the first time. It's a great chance to talk about your daily life in Korean!

CONVERSATION

MP3 74

A 안녕하세요, 지호 씨! 반가워요. 저는 알렉스예요.
Hello, Jiho! Nice to meet you. I'm Alex.

B 안녕하세요, 알렉스 씨! 한국어 잘하시네요!
Hello, Alex! Your Korean is really good!

A 고마워요. 요즘 한국어를 열심히 공부하고 있어요.
Thanks. I've been studying Korean hard these days.

B 그래요? 보통 언제 공부해요?
Really? When do you usually study?

A 아침에 해요.
I study in the morning.

B 와, 부지런하네요!
Wow, you're so diligent!

A 하하, 아니에요.
Haha, no, not really.

Practice Tracker

☐ ☐ ☐

Words & Phrases

요즘 these days

보통 usually

부지런하네요!
└ 부지런하다 to be diligent

Tip!

When someone compliments you, a polite and humble way to respond is **아니에요** (Not at all). In this dialogue, you also hear **고마워요**, which is friendly and used with someone your age or a friend. But in more formal situations, or when talking to someone you don't know well, it's better to say **감사합니다** instead.

STRUCTURE REVIEW

1 Trace over the gray text to get familiar with each sentence. As you write, say the sentences out loud to help with pronunciation and fluency.

A 안녕하세요, 지호 씨! ___반가워요___. ___저는 알렉스예요___.

B 안녕하세요, 알렉스 씨! 한국어 잘하시네요!

A ___고마워요___. 요즘 한국어를 열심히 ___공부하고 있어요___.

B ___그래요___? 보통 ___언제 공부해요___?

A ___아침에 해요___.

B 와, ___부지런하네요___!

A 하하, ___아니에요___.

2 Complete the dialogue using the hint words with the appropriate patterns and particles.

A 안녕하세요, 지호 씨! ______________ (반갑다*). ______________ (저, 알렉스).

B 안녕하세요, 알렉스 씨! ______________ (한국어, 잘하시다)!

A ______________ (고맙다*). 요즘 한국어를 열심히 ______________ (공부하다).

B 그래요? 보통 ______________ (언제, 공부하다)?

A ______________ (아침, 하다).

B 와, ______________ (부지런하다)!

A 하하, 아니에요.

SCENARIO 2

It's Monday, and you're meeting your language exchange partner again. Let's talk about what you did over the weekend in Korean.

CONVERSATION

MP3 75

A 안녕하세요! 주말 잘 보냈어요?
Hi! Did you have a good weekend?

B 네! 한강에서 자전거 탔어요.
Yes! I rode a bike by the Han River.
진짜 재미있었어요.
It was really fun.

A 와, 누구랑 갔어요?
Wow, who did you go with?

B 친구랑 갔어요.
I went with a friend.
친구랑 편의점에서 라면도 먹었어요.
I even had ramyeon with my friend at the convenience store.

A 정말요? 한강 라면 맛있죠?
Really? Ramyeon at the Han River is so good, right?

B 네, 너무 맛있었어요.
Yes, it was so delicious.
다음 주에 또 갈 거예요!
I'm going again next week!

Practice Tracker

☐ ☐ ☐

Words & Phrases

잘 well

한강 Han River

자전거 bike

탔어요
└ 타다 to ride

편의점 convenience store

또 again

Tip!

주말 잘 보냈어요? is a friendly way to ask someone about their weekend, especially on Mondays. You can also use the same pattern for holidays, like: **휴가 잘 보냈어요?** (Did you have a good vacation?) or **크리스마스 잘 보냈어요?** (Did you have a good Christmas?).

STRUCTURE REVIEW

1 Trace over the gray text to get familiar with each sentence. As you write, say the sentences out loud to help with pronunciation and fluency.

A 안녕하세요! 주말 잘 보냈어요?

B 네! 한강에서 자전거 탔어요.

진짜 재미있었어요.

A 와, 누구랑 갔어요?

B 친구랑 갔어요. 친구랑 편의점에서 라면도 먹었어요.

A 정말요? 한강 라면 맛있죠?

B 네, 너무 맛있었어요.

다음 주에 또 갈 거예요!

2 Complete the dialogue using the hint words with the appropriate patterns and particles.

A 안녕하세요! ______________________?
(주말, 잘 보내다)

B 네! 한강에서 ______________________.
(자전거, 타다)

진짜 ______________________.
(재미있다)

A 와, 누구랑 갔어요?

B ______________________. 친구랑 편의점에서 ______________________.
(친구, 가다) (라면, 먹다)

A 정말요? 한강 라면 맛있죠?

B 네, ______________________. ______________________!
(너무, 맛있다) (다음 주, 또 가다)

SCENARIO 3

You get a call from a friend. Let's try a short, friendly call. Talk about your current activity and ask about theirs too.

CONVERSATION

MP3 76

A 여보세요?
Hello?

B 여보세요, 알렉스 씨? 저 지호예요. 지금 뭐 해요?
Hi, Alex. This is Jiho. What are you doing now?

A 안녕하세요, 지호 씨! 저 지금 한국어 숙제하고 있어요.
Hi, Jiho! I'm doing Korean homework right now.

숙제하고 TV 볼 거예요.
I'm going to finish my homework and watch TV.

지호 씨는 뭐 해요?
What about you, Jiho?

B 카페에서 커피 마시고 있어요. 도서관 앞 카페 알아요?
I'm drinking coffee at a café. Do you know the one in front of the library?

A 아니요, 몰라요.
No, I don't know.

B 그래요? 그럼 우리 다음에 같이 와요. 숙제 힘내세요!
Oh really? Then let's come together next time. Good luck with your homework!

A 네, 고마워요!
Thanks!

Practice Tracker

☐ ☐ ☐

Words & Phrases

숙제하고 있어요
└ 숙제 homework
└ 숙제하다 to do homework

도서관 library

다음에 next time

같이 [가치] together

힘내세요! Good luck!, Cheer up!
└ 힘내다 to cheer up

Tip!

힘내세요! is a friendly way to say "Cheer up!" You can just say **힘내세요**, or make it more specific by mentioning what the person is doing, like **숙제 힘내세요!** (Good luck with your homework!) or **한국어 공부 힘내세요!** (Good luck with your Korean studies!). Use it to cheer up your friends or show support in everyday situations.

STRUCTURE REVIEW

1 Trace over the gray text to get familiar with each sentence. As you write, say the sentences out loud to help with pronunciation and fluency.

A 여보세요?

B 여보세요, 알렉스 씨? 저 지호예요. 지금 뭐 해요?

A 안녕하세요, 지호 씨! 저 지금 한국어 숙제하고 있어요.
숙제하고 TV 볼 거예요. 지호 씨는 뭐 해요?

B 카페에서 커피 마시고 있어요. 도서관 앞 카페 알아요?

A 아니요, 몰라요.

B 그래요? 그럼 우리 다음에 같이 와요.
숙제 힘내세요!

A 네, 고마워요!

2 Complete the dialogue using the hint words with the appropriate patterns and particles.

A 여보세요?

B 여보세요, 알렉스 씨? 저 지호예요. ______________?
(지금, 뭐, 하다)

A 안녕하세요, 지호 씨! 저 지금 ______________.
(한국어 숙제하다)

______________. ______________?
(숙제하다 + TV 보다) (지호 씨, 뭐, 하다)

B 카페에서 ______________. 도서관 앞 카페 ______________?
(커피, 마시다) (알다)

A 아니요, ______________.
(모르다)

B 그래요? 그럼 우리 다음에 같이 와요. ______________!
(숙제, 힘내다)

A 네, ______________!
(고맙다)

UNIT 4

Making Plans and Appointments 약속 잡기

Making plans and appointments is a natural way to use Korean in real life. Let's practice how to set up a time to meet, suggest activities, and even cancel politely. Once you're comfortable with the conversation patterns, try changing the time or location to fit new situations.

Key Patterns

- **N이/가 있어요/없어요** PART II - UNIT 4
- **V-(으)세요** PART II - UNIT 18
- **안 A/V, 못 V** PART II - UNIT 11
- **V-(으)ㄹ까요?** PART II - UNIT 20
- **V-아/어도 돼요?** PART II - UNIT 13
- **V-고 싶어요** PART II - UNIT 23

SCENARIO 1

You have a question and want to ask your Korean teacher if they have a moment to talk.

CONVERSATION

MP3 77

A 선생님, 저 질문이 있는데요. 지금 시간 있으세요?
Teacher, I have a question. Do you have a moment?

B 아, 미안해요. 지금 수업이 있어요. 수업 끝나고 봐도 괜찮아요?
Ah, sorry. I have a class now. Is it okay to meet after class?

A 네, 그럼요!
Sure, of course!

B 좋아요. 수업은 1시에 끝나요. 1시에 제 방으로 오세요.
Great. Class ends at 1 o'clock. Come to my office at 1.

A 네, 1시에 선생님 방으로 갈게요. 감사합니다!
Okay, I'll come to your office at 1. Thank you!

B 네, 수업 끝나고 봐요!
Yes. See you after class!

Practice Tracker

☐ ☐ ☐

Words & Phrases

질문 question

수업 끝나고 봐도 괜찮아요?
└ 수업 class
└ 끝나다 to end
└ 보다 to meet

방 room

Tip!

In **수업 끝나고 봐도 돼요?** and **수업 끝나고 봐요!**, **-고** is used to connect two actions or states. It can mean "and" or "after," depending on context. You can use it to list actions or show the order. Just add **-고** directly to the stem of a verb or adjective—no need to worry about **받침** (final consonant).

STRUCTURE REVIEW

1 Trace over the gray text to get familiar with each sentence. As you write, say the sentences out loud to help with pronunciation and fluency.

A 선생님, 저 질문이 있는데요.
지금 시간 있으세요?

B 아, 미안해요. 지금 수업이 있어요.
수업 끝나고 봐도 괜찮아요?

A 네, 그럼요!

B 좋아요. 수업은 1시에 끝나요.
1시에 제 방으로 오세요.

A 네, 1시에 선생님 방으로 갈게요. 감사합니다!

B 네, 수업 끝나고 봐요!

2 Complete the dialogue using the hint words with the appropriate patterns and particles.

A 선생님, 저 ______________________. (질문, 있다)
지금 시간 있으세요?

B 아, 미안해요. ______________________. (지금, 수업, 있다)
수업 끝나고 봐도 괜찮아요?

A 네, 그럼요!

B 좋아요. 수업은 ______________________. (1시, 끝나다)
1시에 제 방으로 ______________. (오다)

A 네, 1시에 선생님 방으로 ______________. (가다) 감사합니다!

B 네, 수업 끝나고 봐요!

SCENARIO 2

You and your friend like the same actor. A new movie starring that actor just came out. Suggest watching it together and make a plan.

CONVERSATION

MP3 78

A 알렉스 씨, 톰 크루즈 새 영화가 나왔어요. 같이 볼래요?
Alex, the new Tom Cruise movie is out. Want to watch it together?

B 와 정말요? 보고 싶어요! 내일 시간 돼요?
Wow, really? I want to see it! Are you free tomorrow?

A 아, 내일은 약속이 있어요. 내일모레 어때요?
Oh, I have an appointment tomorrow. How about the day after tomorrow?

B 내일모레 좋아요. 몇 시에 만날까요?
The day after tomorrow works. What time should we meet?

A 세 시 어때요?
How about 3 o'clock?

B 세 시 좋아요. 어디에서 만날까요?
Sounds good. Where should we meet?

A 영화관 앞에서 만날까요?
Shall we meet in front of the theater?

B 네. 그럼 세 시에 영화관 앞에서 만나요.
Okay. Let's meet in front of the theater at 3, then.

A 네, 그때 봐요!
Alright, see you then!

Practice Tracker

□ □ □

Words & Phrases

새 new

나왔어요
└, 나오다 to come out

약속 appointment

내일모레 어때요?
└, N 어때요? How about N?

영화관 movie theater

그때 then (that time)

Tip!

The pattern N **어때요?** means "How about ~?" or "What do you think about ~?" You can use it to ask someone's opinion or gently make a suggestion, like in **내일모레 어때요?** or **세 시 어때요?** It's simple, polite, and useful in many everyday situations.

STRUCTURE REVIEW

1 Trace over the gray text to get familiar with each sentence. As you write, say the sentences out loud to help with pronunciation and fluency.

A 알렉스 씨, 톰 크루즈 새 영화가 나왔어요. 같이 볼래요?

B 와 정말요? 보고 싶어요! 내일 시간 돼요?

A 아, 내일은 약속이 있어요. 내일모레 어때요?

B 내일모레 좋아요. 몇 시에 만날까요?

A 세 시 어때요?

B 세 시 좋아요. 어디에서 만날까요?

A 영화관 앞에서 만날까요?

B 네. 그럼 세 시에 영화관 앞에서 만나요.

A 네, 그때 봐요!

2 Complete the dialogue using the hint words with the appropriate patterns and particles.

A 알렉스 씨, 톰 크루즈 새 영화가 나왔어요. 같이 볼래요?

B 와 정말요? ______________ ! ______________ ?
(보다) (내일, 시간, 되다)

A 아, 내일은 ______________ . 내일모레 어때요?
(약속, 있다)

B 내일모레 좋아요. ______________ ?
(몇 시, 만나다)

A 세 시 어때요?

B 세 시 좋아요. ______________ ?
(어디, 만나다)

A 영화관 앞에서 만날까요?

B 네. 그럼 ______________ .
(세 시, 영화관 앞, 만나다)

A 네, 그때 봐요!

SCENARIO 3

You made plans with a friend, but now you feel sick and think you caught a cold. Call your friend to explain and try to reschedule.

CONVERSATION

MP3 79

A 여보세요, 지호 씨? 미안해요. 오늘 못 만날 것 같아요.
Hello, Jiho? Sorry, I don't think I can make it today.

B 왜요? 무슨 일 있어요?
Why? Is there something wrong?

A 감기에 걸렸어요.
I caught a cold.

B 아이고, 괜찮아요?
Oh no, are you okay?

A 네, 그런데 집에서 좀 쉬고 싶어요.
Yes, but I want to rest at home for a while.

B 그래요. 우리 영화는 다음에 봐요.
Okay. Let's watch the movie next time.

A 네, 제가 다시 연락할게요. 정말 미안해요.
Sure, I'll contact you again. I'm really sorry.

B 아니에요. 푹 쉬세요!
No problem. Rest well!

A 네, 고마워요.
Okay, thank you.

Practice Tracker

☐ ☐ ☐

Words & Phrases

못 만날 것 같아요
└ 못 V-(으)ㄹ 것 같아요
I don't think I can ~

무슨 일 있어요?
Is there something wrong?

집 home

좀 쉬고 싶어요
└ 좀 a little, a bit
└ 쉬다 to rest

다시 again

연락할게요 [연라칼께요]
└ 연락하다 to contact

푹 쉬세요! Rest well!
└ 푹 fully

Tip!

When you want to politely cancel plans, **못 만날 것 같아요** sounds softer than just saying **못 만나요**. This phrase uses the **-(으)ㄹ 것 같아요** pattern, which means "I think it will ~." It shows that meeting is probably difficult, even if you want to.

STRUCTURE REVIEW

1 **Trace over the gray text to get familiar with each sentence. As you write, say the sentences out loud to help with pronunciation and fluency.**

A 여보세요, 지호 씨? 미안해요. 오늘 못 만날 것 같아요.

B 왜요? 무슨 일 있어요?

A 감기에 걸렸어요.

B 아이고, 괜찮아요?

A 네, 그런데 집에서 좀 쉬고 싶어요.

B 그래요. 우리 영화는 다음에 봐요.

A 네, 제가 다시 연락할게요. 정말 미안해요.

B 아니에요. 푹 쉬세요!

A 네, 고마워요.

2 **Complete the dialogue using the hint words with the appropriate patterns and particles.**

A 여보세요, 지호 씨? 미안해요. 오늘 못 만날 것 같아요.

B 왜요? ______________________?
(무슨 일, 있다)

A ______________________.
(감기에 걸리다)

B 아이고, 괜찮아요?

A 네, 그런데 ______________________.
(집, 좀, 쉬다)

B 그래요. 우리 영화는 다음에 봐요.

A 네, 제가 ______________________. 정말 미안해요.
(다시 연락하다)

B 아니에요. ______________________!
(푹 쉬다)

A 네, 고마워요.

UNIT 5 At a Café 카페 이용하기

If you visit Korea, don't miss the chance to enjoy all kinds of cafés-from cozy local shops to big chain cafés. To enjoy them fully, you'll need to know how to order drinks, ask for Wi-Fi or the bathroom, and say "for here" or "to go."

Key Patterns

- **N이/가 있어요/없어요** PART II - UNIT 4
- **N이에요/예요** PART II - UNIT 5
- **V-아/어 주세요** PART II - UNIT 12
- **V-아/어도 돼요?** PART II - UNIT 13
- **V-(으)세요** PART II - UNIT 18

SCENARIO 1

It's a rainy afternoon and you drop by a cozy café. Let's try ordering a hot drink and a piece of cake.

CONVERSATION

MP3 80

A 안녕하세요. 따뜻한 아메리카노 하나 주세요.
Hello. One hot Americano, please.

B 네, 드시고 가세요?
Sure, is this for here?

A 네. 아, 초코 케이크도 하나 주세요.
Yes. Oh, and one chocolate cake, please.

B 따뜻한 아메리카노하고 초코 케이크, 맞으세요?
One hot Americano and one chocolate cake, right?

A 네, 맞아요.
That's right.

B 네, 만 원입니다.
That'll be 10,000 won.

A 여기 있어요.
Here you go.

B 감사합니다, Thank you.
준비되면 알려 드릴게요.
We'll let you know when it's ready.

Practice Tracker

☐ ☐ ☐

Words & Phrases

따뜻한 [따뜨탄] 아메리카노
hot Americano
└, 따뜻하다 [따뜨타다] to be warm

드시고 가세요? For here?

초코 케이크 chocolate cake

맞으세요?
└, 맞다 to be right/correct

준비되면 알려 드릴게요 [드릴께요]
└, 준비되다 to be ready
└, 알려 드리다 to let someone know (honorific form of 알려 주다)

Tip!

When speaking politely to someone like a customer, teacher, or elder, **주다** changes to **드리다**, so you'll often hear phrases like **알려 드릴게요** (I'll let you know) or **가져다드릴게요** (I'll bring it to you). The ending **-(으)ㄹ게요** means "I will ~" as a promise or quick decision to the listener. We covered this alongside **-(으)ㄹ거예요** in *Part II, Unit 21*—check it out if you'd like a review!

STRUCTURE REVIEW

1 **Trace over the gray text to get familiar with each sentence. As you write, say the sentences out loud to help with pronunciation and fluency.**

A 안녕하세요. 따뜻한 아메리카노 하나 주세요.

B 네, 드시고 가세요?

A 네. 아, 초코 케이크도 하나 주세요.

B 따뜻한 아메리카노하고 초코 케이크, 맞으세요?

A 네, 맞아요.

B 네, 만 원입니다.

A 여기 있어요.

B 감사합니다, 준비되면 알려 드릴게요.

2 **Complete the dialogue using the hint words with the appropriate patterns and particles.**

A 안녕하세요. ______________________.
(따뜻한 아메리카노, 하나, 주다)

B 네, 드시고 가세요?

A 네. 아, ______________________.
(초코 케이크, 하나, 주다)

B 따뜻한 아메리카노하고 초코 케이크, 맞으세요?

A 네, ______________.
(맞다)

B 네, 만 원입니다.

A 여기 있어요.

B 감사합니다, 준비되면 ______________________.
(알려 드리다)

SCENARIO 2

You're staying at the café and want to connect to the Wi-Fi. You also need to use the bathroom, but both the Wi-Fi and restroom require passwords. Let's go to the counter and ask.

CONVERSATION

MP3 81

A 저, 죄송한데 와이파이 비밀번호가 뭐예요?
Excuse me, what's the Wi-Fi password?

B 여기 영수증에 있어요.
It's on your receipt.

A 아, 감사합니다. 그리고 혹시 화장실 좀 써도 될까요?
Ah, thank you. Also, may I use the restroom?

B 그럼요. 화장실 비밀번호는 3537이에요.
Of course. The restroom password is 3537.

A 감사합니다.
Thank you.

Practice Tracker

☐ ☐ ☐

Words & Phrases

비밀번호 password

영수증 receipt

Tip!

써도 될까요? is a polite way to ask "May I use it?" You can also say **써도 돼요?** with the same meaning.
In many Korean cafés, the Wi-Fi and restroom require passwords. Sometimes, the Wi-Fi password is posted somewhere inside.

STRUCTURE REVIEW

1 Trace over the gray text to get familiar with each sentence. As you write, say the sentences out loud to help with pronunciation and fluency.

A 저, 죄송한데 __와이파이 비밀번호가 뭐예요__?

B 여기 __영수증에 있어요__.

A 아, 감사합니다.

그리고 혹시 __화장실 좀 써도 될까요__?

B 그럼요. __화장실 비밀번호는 3537이에요__.

A 감사합니다.

2 Complete the dialogue using the hint words with the appropriate patterns and particles.

A 저, 죄송한데 ____________________?
(와이파이 비밀번호, 뭐)

B 여기 ____________________.
(영수증, 있다)

A 아, 감사합니다.

그리고 혹시 ____________________?
(화장실, 좀 쓰다)

B 그럼요. 화장실 비밀번호는 3537이에요.

A 감사합니다.

SCENARIO 3

You're on your way to meet a friend and want to bring some refreshing iced lattes to enjoy together. You stop by a café to order two iced lattes to go.

CONVERSATION

MP3 82

A 안녕하세요. 아이스라테 두 잔 주세요.
Hello. Two iced lattes, please.

B 드시고 가세요?
For here?

A 아니요, 테이크아웃이요.
No, to go.

B 네, 아이스라테 포장이요. 5,000원입니다.
Okay, iced latte to go. That's 5,000 won.

A 여기 있어요.
Here you go.

B 네, 영수증 필요하세요?
Sure, would you like a receipt?

A 아니요, 버려 주세요.
No, please throw it away.

B 네, 이쪽에서 잠시만 기다려 주세요.
Sure, please wait over here for a moment.

A 네, 감사합니다.
Okay. Thanks.

Practice Tracker

☐ ☐ ☐

Words & Phrases

아이스라테 iced latte

포장 takeout, to-go

필요하세요?
└ 필요하다 to need

버려 주세요
└ 버리다 to throw away

이쪽 over here

Tip!

In many stores, receipts and bags are not always given automatically. You'll often hear **영수증 필요하세요?** (Do you need a receipt?) or **영수증 드릴까요?** (Shall I give you the receipt?). If you don't want it, you can politely say **버려 주세요** (Please throw it away). And if you want the receipt, you can ask **영수증 주세요** (Please give me the receipt).

STRUCTURE REVIEW

1 Trace over the gray text to get familiar with each sentence. As you write, say the sentences out loud to help with pronunciation and fluency.

A 안녕하세요. 아이스라테 두 잔 주세요.

B 드시고 가세요?

A 아니요, 테이크아웃이요.

B 네, 아이스라테 포장이요. 5,000원입니다.

A 여기 있어요.

B 네, 영수증 필요하세요?

A 아니요, 버려 주세요.

B 네, 이쪽에서 잠시만 기다려 주세요.

A 네, 감사합니다.

2 Complete the dialogue using the hint words with the appropriate patterns and particles.

A 안녕하세요. ______________________________.
(아이스라테 두 잔, 주다)

B 드시고 가세요?

A 아니요, ______________________.
(테이크아웃)

B 네, 아이스라테 포장이요. 5,000원입니다.

A 여기 있어요.

B 네, ______________________________?
(영수증, 필요하다)

A 아니요, ______________________.
(버리다)

B 네, 이쪽에서 잠시만 기다려 주세요.

A 네, 감사합니다.

UNIT 6

At a Restaurant 식당 이용하기

Eating out at **식당** (restaurant) in Korea is easy and fun. Let's get ready to enjoy Korean food like a local. In this unit, you can practice how to order, enjoy your meal, and pay politely.

Key Patterns

- **N이에요/예요** PART II - UNIT 5
- **V-(으)세요** PART II - UNIT 18
- **A/V-아/어요** PART II - UNIT 10
- **V-(으)ㄹ 수 있어요** PART II - UNIT 22
- **N 주세요** PART II - UNIT 12
- **V-고 싶어요** PART II - UNIT 23

SCENARIO 1

Let's try going to a Korean restaurant alone! It might sound a little difficult at first, but it's actually quite simple.

CONVERSATION

MP3 83

A 어서 오세요. 몇 분이세요?
Welcome. How many people?

B 한 명이에요.
Just one, please.

A 네, 저쪽에 앉으세요.
Okay, please sit over there.

(After sitting down)

B 여기요, 불고기 1인분 주문할 수 있어요?
Excuse me, can I order only one serving of bulgogi?

A 네, 1인분 돼요.
Yes, that's possible.

B 그럼 불고기 1인분 주세요.
Then I'll have one serving of bulgogi, please.

A 네, 잠깐만 기다리세요.
Sure, just a moment.

Practice Tracker

☐ ☐ ☐

Words & Phrases

몇 분이세요? How many people?

저쪽 over there

불고기 bulgogi

1인분 [이린분] one serving

주문할 수 있어요?
[주문할 쑤 이써요]
└ 주문하다 to order

Tip!

Servings are counted with **Sino-Korean numbers + 인분** (serving): **1인분 (일 인분)**, **2인분 (이 인분)**, and so on. For some dishes like barbecue or hot pot, you may need to order at least two servings. If you're eating alone, ask: **1인분 돼요?**

STRUCTURE REVIEW

1 Trace over the gray text to get familiar with each sentence. As you write, say the sentences out loud to help with pronunciation and fluency.

A 어서 오세요. 몇 분이세요?

B 한 명이에요.

A 네, 저쪽에 앉으세요.

(After sitting down)

B 여기요, 불고기 1인분 주문할 수 있어요?

A 네, 1인분 돼요.

B 그럼 불고기 1인분 주세요.

A 네, 잠깐만 기다리세요.

2 Complete the dialogue using the hint words with the appropriate patterns and particles.

A 어서 오세요. ________________? (몇 분)

B ________________. (한 명)

A 네, ________________. (저쪽, 앉다)

(After sitting down)

B 여기요, ________________? (불고기 1인분, 주문하다)

A 네, 1인분 돼요.

B 그럼 ________________. (불고기 1인분, 주다)

A 네, 잠깐만 기다리세요.

SCENARIO 2

You and a friend are looking at the menu together. You talk about what to eat, ask if a dish is spicy, and decide to order two dishes to share.

CONVERSATION

MP3 84

A 제이드 씨, 뭐 먹고 싶어요? 여기는 순두부찌개가 맛있어요.
Jade, what do you want to eat? The soft tofu stew here is good.

B 오, 여기 순두부찌개 맛집이에요? 저 순두부찌개 좋아해요!
Oh, is this place known for soft tofu stew? I like soft tofu stew.

아, 그런데 비빔밥도 있네요.
Ah, but they have bibimbap too.

A 여기 비빔밥도 맛있어요. 비빔밥 먹을래요?
The bibimbap here is good too. Do you want to have bibimbap?

B 어떡하죠? 순두부찌개도 먹고 싶고, 비빔밥도 먹고 싶어요.
What should I do? I want to have both the soft tofu stew and the bibimbap.

A 저도요! 그럼 우리 비빔밥 하나, 순두부찌개 하나 시켜요.
Me too! Then let's order one bibimbap and one soft tofu stew.

같이 먹어요.
We can share.

B 와, 좋아요!
Wow, sounds great!

A 여기요! 비빔밥 하나, 순두부찌개 하나 주세요.
Excuse me! One bibimbap and one soft tofu stew, please.

앞접시도 주세요.
And some small plates too, please.

Practice Tracker

☐ ☐ ☐

Words & Phrases

순두부찌개 soft tofu stew

맛집 famous food spot

비빔밥 [비빔빱] bibimbap

어떡하죠? [어떠카죠]
What should I do?

시켜요
└ 시키다 to order

앞접시 small individual plate
(for sharing food)

Tip!

Going out to eat with friends and looking for **맛집** (famous food spots) is a fun part of life in Korea. Since people often want to try different dishes, they usually order a few things and share. When sharing food, it's common to ask for **앞접시** (small plates) so everyone can have their own portion.

STRUCTURE REVIEW

1 Trace over the gray text to get familiar with each sentence. As you write, say the sentences out loud to help with pronunciation and fluency.

A 제이드 씨, 뭐 먹고 싶어요?
여기는 순두부찌개가 맛있어요.

B 오, 여기 순두부찌개 맛집이에요? 저 순두부찌개 좋아해요!
아, 그런데 비빔밥도 있네요.

A 여기 비빔밥도 맛있어요. 비빔밥 먹을래요?

B 어떡하죠? 순두부찌개도 먹고 싶고, 비빔밥도 먹고 싶어요.

A 저도요! 그럼 우리 비빔밥 하나, 순두부찌개 하나 시켜요. 같이 먹어요.

B 와, 좋아요!

A 여기요! 비빔밥 하나, 순두부찌개 하나 주세요. 앞접시도 주세요.

2 Complete the dialogue using the hint words with the appropriate patterns and particles.

A 제이드 씨, ______________? 여기는 순두부찌개가 맛있어요.
(뭐, 먹다)

B 오, 여기 순두부찌개 맛집이에요? ______________!
(저, 순두부찌개, 좋아하다)
아, 그런데 비빔밥도 있네요.

A 여기 비빔밥도 맛있어요. ______________?
(비빔밥, 먹다)

B 어떡하죠? 순두부찌개도 먹고 싶고, 비빔밥도 먹고 싶어요.

A 저도요! 그럼 우리 비빔밥 하나, 순두부 찌개 하나 시켜요. ______________.
(같이, 먹다)

B 와, 좋아요!

A 여기요! ______________.
(비빔밥 하나, 순두부찌개 하나, 주다)
______________.
(앞접시, 주다)

SCENARIO 3

In Korean restaurants, you usually pay at the counter, not at the table. Let's practice paying the bill in Korean.

CONVERSATION

MP3 85

A 여기요, 계산해 주세요.
I'd like to pay, please.

B 네, 27,000원입니다.
Sure, that's 27,000 won.

A 카드로 할게요.
I'll pay by card.

B 네. 식사 맛있게 하셨어요?
Okay. Did you enjoy your meal?

A 네, 정말 맛있었어요!
Yes, it was really delicious!

B 감사합니다. 영수증 여기 있어요.
Thank you. Here's your receipt.

A 네. 잘 먹었습니다. 안녕히 계세요.
Thanks. I really enjoyed the meal. Goodbye.

B 안녕히 가세요! 또 오세요!
Goodbye! Please come again!

Practice Tracker

☐ ☐ ☐

Words & Phrases

카드로 할게요 [할께요]
↳ N(으)로 할게요 I'll pay ~ by/with N

식사 맛있게 하셨어요?
Did you enjoy your meal?
↳ 식사 meal

또 오세요! Please come again!
↳ 또 again
↳ 오다 to come

Tip!

In Korea, when you go to pay after a meal, the staff might ask if you enjoyed your meal. It's a polite and friendly way to check if everything was okay. You can simply answer with **네** or say **맛있었어요** (It was delicious).

STRUCTURE REVIEW

1 Trace over the gray text to get familiar with each sentence. As you write, say the sentences out loud to help with pronunciation and fluency.

A 여기요, ___계산해 주세요___.

B 네, 27,000원입니다.

A ___카드로 할게요___.

B 네. 식사 맛있게 하셨어요?

A ___네, 정말 맛있었어요!___!

B 감사합니다. 영수증 여기 있어요.

A 네. ___잘 먹었습니다___. ___안녕히 계세요___.

B 안녕히 가세요! ___또 오세요___!

2 Complete the dialogue using the hint words with the appropriate patterns and particles.

A 여기요, ________________.
(계산하다)

B 네, 27,000원입니다.

A ________________.
(카드, 하다)

B 네. 식사 맛있게 하셨어요?

A 네, ________________!
(정말, 맛있다)

B 감사합니다. 영수증 여기 있어요.

A 네. ________________. 안녕히 계세요.
(잘, 먹다)

B 안녕히 가세요! ________________!
(또, 오다)

UNIT 7

At a Convenience Store and a Supermarket 편의점 & 마트 이용하기

편의점 (convenience stores) and **마트** (supermarkets) are fun to explore—with 1+1 deals, seasonal snacks, and even places to eat on-site. Supermarkets offer more variety at better prices. Let's practice asking where things are, how much they cost, and how to pay!

Key Patterns

- **N이/가 있어요/없어요** PART II - UNIT 4
- **N이에요/예요** PART II - UNIT 5
- **V-아/어 주세요, N 주세요** PART II - UNIT 12
- **V-아/어도 돼요?** PART II - UNIT 13
- **A/V-네요** PART II - UNIT 16

SCENARIO 1

Let's try buying some items in Korean. Imagine picking up items and going to the counter to pay. It's easier than you think!

CONVERSATION

MP3 86

A 안녕하세요. 계산해 주세요.
Hello. I'd like to pay, please.

B 네, 13,200원입니다. 봉투 필요하세요?
Sure, that's 13,200 won. Do you need a bag?

A 아니요, 괜찮아요. 카드로 할게요.
No, I'm okay. I'll pay by card.

영수증도 주세요.
Please give me the receipt too.

B 네, 여기 있습니다.
Sure. Here you go.

A 감사합니다. 안녕히 계세요.
Thank you. Goodbye.

B 네, 안녕히 가세요!
Goodbye!

Practice Tracker

☐ ☐ ☐

Words & Phrases

봉투 plastic/paper bag

Tip!

편의점 (convenience store) is a small shop open 24/7, perfect for quick snacks, drinks, and daily essentials. **마트** (mart or supermarket) is larger, offering a wider selection of groceries and household items at lower prices. Many stores now have self-checkout machines for faster service.

STRUCTURE REVIEW

1 Trace over the gray text to get familiar with each sentence. As you write, say the sentences out loud to help with pronunciation and fluency.

A 안녕하세요. 계산해 주세요.

B 네, 13,200원입니다. 봉투 필요하세요?

A 아니요, 괜찮아요. 카드로 할게요.
영수증도 주세요.

B 네, 여기 있습니다.

A 감사합니다. 안녕히 계세요.

B 네, 안녕히 가세요!

2 Complete the dialogue using the hint words with the appropriate patterns and particles.

A 안녕하세요. ____________________.
(계산하다)

B 네, 13,200원입니다. ____________________?
(봉투, 필요하다)

A 아니요, ____________________. ____________________.
(괜찮다) (카드, 하다)

____________________.
(영수증, 주다)

B 네, 여기 있습니다.

A 감사합니다. ____________________.
(안녕히, 계시다)

B 네, ____________________!
(안녕히, 가다)

SCENARIO 2

Let's go to the supermarket. It's bigger than a convenience store, so you might need to ask where things are or how much they cost. Let's practice asking the staff.

CONVERSATION

MP3 87

A 저기요, 죄송한데 시리얼이 어디 있어요?
Excuse me, where is the cereal?

B 아, 저기 라면 코너 옆에 있어요.
Oh, it's next to the ramyeon section over there.

저쪽에 라면 보이죠?
Do you see the ramyeon section over there?

A 네, 보여요. 감사합니다!
Yes, I see it. Thank you!

(A little later)

A 혹시 이거 얼마예요?
Excuse me, how much is this?

B 음, 잠시만요. 6,000원이네요.
Just a moment... Oh, that's 6,000 won.

A 네, 감사합니다!
Okay, thank you!

Practice Tracker

☐ ☐ ☐

Words & Phrases

시리얼 cereal

코너 section/area in a store

보이죠?, 보여요
└ 보이다 to be visible

Tip!

In Korean stores, people often say **OO 코너** to talk about different sections, like **라면 코너** (ramyeon section), **과자 코너** (snack section), or **음료 코너** (beverage section). It's a common way to describe areas inside a store.

STRUCTURE REVIEW

1 Trace over the gray text to get familiar with each sentence. As you write, say the sentences out loud to help with pronunciation and fluency.

A 저기요, 죄송한데 시리얼이 어디 있어요?

B 아, 저기 라면 코너 옆에 있어요.

저쪽에 라면 보이죠?

A 네, 보여요. 감사합니다!

(A little later)

A 혹시 이거 얼마예요?

B 음, 잠시만요. 6,000원이네요.

A 네, 감사합니다!

2 Complete the dialogue using the hint words with the appropriate patterns and particles.

A 저기요, 죄송한데 ______________________________?
(시리얼, 어디, 있다)

B 아, 저기 ______________________________.
(라면 코너 옆, 있다)

저쪽에 ______________?
(라면, 보이다)

A 네, ______________________. 감사합니다!
(보이다)

(A little later)

A 혹시 ______________________?
(이거, 얼마)

B 음, 잠시만요. 6,000원이네요.

A 네, 감사합니다!

SCENARIO 3

Many Korean convenience stores have hot water, microwaves, and even tables, so you can enjoy your food right away. Let's try it! Pick what you want, go to the counter, and ask if you can eat there.

CONVERSATION

MP3 88

A 안녕하세요. 이거 계산해 주세요.
Hello. I'd like to pay for this, please.

B 네, 2,000원입니다.
Sure, that's 2,000 won.

A 여기 있어요. 여기에서 컵라면 먹어도 돼요?
Here you go. Is it okay to have cup noodles here?

B 네, 드셔도 돼요. 뜨거운 물은 저기에 있어요.
Yes, you can. The hot water is over there.

A 아, 감사합니다. 저기 테이블에 앉아도 돼요?
Ah, thank you. May I sit at that table over there?

B 네, 그럼요. 젓가락도 가져가세요. 여기 있어요.
Of course. Take some chopsticks, too. Here you go.

A 감사합니다.
Thank you.

Practice Tracker

☐ ☐ ☐

Words & Phrases

컵라면 instant cup noodles

뜨거운 물 hot water
└ 물 water

젓가락 chopsticks

가져가세요
└ 가져가다 to take (with someone)

Tip!

In many Korean convenience stores, there are small tables inside or outside where you can eat food right after buying it. But not all stores allow it, so if you're not sure, you can ask: **여기서/저기서 먹어도 돼요?** (Is it okay to eat here/over there?)

STRUCTURE REVIEW

1 Trace over the gray text to get familiar with each sentence. As you write, say the sentences out loud to help with pronunciation and fluency.

A 안녕하세요. 이거 계산해 주세요.

B 네, 2,000원입니다.

A 여기 있어요. 여기에서 컵라면 먹어도 돼요?

B 네, 드셔도 돼요. 뜨거운 물은 저기에 있어요.

A 아, 감사합니다. 저기 테이블에 앉아도 돼요?

B 네, 그럼요. 젓가락도 가져가세요. 여기 있어요.

A 감사합니다.

2 Complete the dialogue using the hint words with the appropriate patterns and particles.

A 안녕하세요. ________________.
(이거, 계산하다)

B 네, 2,000원입니다.

A 여기 있어요. ________________?
(여기, 컵라면, 먹다)

B 네, 드셔도 돼요. ________________.
(뜨거운 물, 저기, 있다)

A 아, 감사합니다. 저기 테이블에 ________________?
(앉다)

B 네, 그럼요. 젓가락도 ________________. 여기 있어요.
(가져가다)

A 감사합니다.

UNIT 8

Shopping at a Market 시장 이용하기

Visiting **시장** (traditional market) is a great way to try street food, fresh fruit, and local items—and to use your Korean in real conversations. Let's learn how to ask questions, order, and chat with vendors.

Key Patterns

- **N이에요/예요** PART II - UNIT 5
- **안 A/V, 못 V** PART II - UNIT 11
- **N 주세요** PART II - UNIT 12
- **V-아/어도 돼요?** PART II - UNIT 13
- **V-지 마세요** PART II - UNIT 19
- **A-(으)ㄴ데요, V-는데요** PART II - UNIT 25

SCENARIO 1

Korean markets are full of tasty street food. Some of them have funny or surprising names! Let's ask what this food is and give it a try.

CONVERSATION

MP3 89

A 사장님, '떡튀순'이 뭐예요?
Excuse me, sir, what does "떡튀순" mean?

B 아, 떡튀순이요? 떡볶이, 튀김, 순대 세트예요.
Oh, 떡튀순? It's a set of tteokbokki, twigim, and soondae.

떡볶이의 떡, 튀김의 튀, 순대의 순!
"떡" from 떡볶이, "튀" from 튀김, and "순" from 순대!

그래서 떡튀순이에요. 재미있죠?
So it's "떡튀순." Funny, right?

A 그렇군요. 재미있네요! 사진 찍어도 돼요?
Oh, I see. That's interesting! May I take a photo?

B 그럼요! 찍으세요.
Sure! Go ahead.

A 감사합니다. 떡튀순 1인분 주세요. 여기에서 먹을게요.
Thank you. One order of 떡튀순, please. I'll eat here.

B 네, 이쪽에 앉으세요.
Sure, have a seat here.

Practice Tracker

☐ ☐ ☐

Words & Phrases

김밥 [김빱] gimbap

떡볶이 tteokbokki

순대 soondae (Korean blood sausage)

튀김 twigim (Korean-style deep-fried snacks)

Tip!

In markets or small shops, people often say **사장님** (which means "president of the company") to politely call a worker, even if they are not the actual owner. People often make short and fun names by combining the first sounds of words, like **떡튀순** (tteokbokki + twigim + soondae) or **치맥** (chicken + beer). Try looking for more food nicknames in Korea!

STRUCTURE REVIEW

1 Trace over the gray text to get familiar with each sentence. As you write, say the sentences out loud to help with pronunciation and fluency.

A 사장님, 떡튀순이 뭐예요?

B 아, 떡튀순이요? 떡볶이, 튀김, 순대 세트예요. 떡볶이의 떡, 튀김의 튀, 순대의 순!
그래서 떡튀순이에요. 재미있죠?

A 그렇군요. 재미있네요! 사진 찍어도 돼요?

B 그럼요! 찍으세요.

A 감사합니다. 떡튀순 1인분 주세요.
여기에서 먹을게요.

B 네, 이쪽에 앉으세요.

2 Complete the dialogue using the hint words with the appropriate patterns and particles.

A 사장님, ____________________?
(떡튀순, 뭐)

B 아, 떡튀순이요? 떡볶이, 튀김, 순대 세트예요. 떡볶이의 떡, 튀김의 튀, 순대의 순!
그래서 떡튀순이에요. ____________________?
(재미있다)

A 그렇군요. 재미있네요! ____________________?
(사진 찍다)

B 그럼요! ____________________.
(찍다)

A 감사합니다. ____________________.
(떡튀순 1인분, 주다)

____________________.
(여기, 먹다)

B 네, ____________________.
(이쪽, 앉다)

SCENARIO 2

When you visit another country, you might come across fruits you've never seen before. Let's ask the vendor what this fruit is and try a bite! Who knows? You might find your new favorite fruit and get to use your Korean in real life.

CONVERSATION

MP3 90

A 사장님, 이 과일 이름이 뭐예요?
Excuse me, what is the name of this fruit?

B 참외예요. 한국 여름 과일이에요.
It's chamoe. It's a Korean summer fruit.

A 맛있어요?
Is it delicious?

B 네, 달고 시원해요.
Yes, it's sweet and refreshing.

A 셔요?
Is it sour?

B 아니요, 안 셔요.
No, it's not sour.

A 그럼 두 개 주세요. 카드 돼요?
Then I'll take two. Can I use a card?

B 그럼요. 4,000원이에요.
Sure. It's 4,000 won.
이건 서비스예요. 하나 더 드릴게요.
This one's on the house. I'll give you one more.

A 와, 감사합니다!
Wow, thank you!

Practice Tracker

☐ ☐ ☐

Words & Phrases

과일 fruit

참외 chamoe (Korean melon)

여름 summer

달고 시원해요
└ 달다 to be sweet
└ 시원하다 to be refreshing/cool

셔요?
└ 시다 to be sour

서비스 something free, service

드릴게요 [드릴께요]
└ 드리다 to give (humble form)

Tip!

At markets or restaurants, **서비스** often means a free gift—like an extra item or side dish. It's one of the fun parts of shopping at markets or eating out. If someone says **서비스예요**, they're giving you something for free. But it can also mean regular service, like in **룸 서비스** (room service) or **고객 서비스** (customer service).

STRUCTURE REVIEW

1 Trace over the gray text to get familiar with each sentence. As you write, say the sentences out loud to help with pronunciation and fluency.

A 사장님, 이 과일 이름이 뭐예요?

B 참외예요. 한국 여름 과일이에요.

A 맛있어요?

B 네, 달고 시원해요.

A 셔요?

B 아니요, 안 셔요.

A 그럼 두 개 주세요. 카드 돼요?

B 그럼요. 4,000원이에요. 이건 서비스예요. 하나 더 드릴게요.

A 와, 감사합니다!

2 Complete the dialogue using the hint words with the appropriate patterns and particles.

A 사장님, ____________________?
(이 과일, 이름, 뭐)

B 참외예요. 한국 여름 과일이에요.

A ____________________?
(맛있다)

B 네, ____________________.
(달다 + 시원하다)

A 셔요?

B 아니요, ____________________.
(X 시다)

A 그럼 ____________________. 카드 돼요?
(두 개, 주다)

B 그럼요. 4,000원이에요. 이건 서비스예요. ____________________.
(하나 더, 드리다)

A 와, 감사합니다!

SCENARIO 3

You're at a market stand that sells many kinds of jeon (Korean pancakes). You want to try kimchi jeon, but you're not sure which one it is. Ask the vendor about it, check if it has anything you can't eat, and order one to go. Good luck!

CONVERSATION

MP3 91

A 사장님, 김치전이 어떤 거예요?
Excuse me, which one is the kimchi pancake?

B 이거예요. 맛있어요.
This one. It's tasty.

A 매워요? 저는 매운 음식을 못 먹어요.
Is it spicy? I can't eat spicy food.

B 하하, 괜찮아요. 이건 많이 안 매워요.
Haha, it's okay. This is not too spicy.

A 아, 그리고 제가 땅콩 알레르기가 있는데요.
Oh, and I have a peanut allergy.

B 아이고, 그래요? 땅콩은 안 들어갔어요. 걱정하지 마세요.
Oh, you do? It doesn't have peanuts. Don't worry.

A 다행이네요! 그럼 하나 포장해 주세요.
That's a relief! Then, please pack one to take away.

B 네. 잠깐만 기다리세요.
Sure. Please wait a moment.

Practice Tracker

☐ ☐ ☐

Words & Phrases

김치전 kimchi pancake

어떤 거 which one

김치가 들어갔어요?
└ 들어가다 to be included

매운 음식 spicy food
└ 맵다 to be spicy
└ 음식 food

땅콩 peanut

알레르기 allergy

걱정하지 마세요
└ 걱정하다 to worry

다행이네요!
└ 다행이다 to be a relief

포장해 주세요
└ 포장하다 to wrap it to go

Tip!

전 is a Korean-style savory pancake (not sweet). It's similar to fritters or omelettes, but lighter and less greasy. It's made by pan-frying ingredients such as kimchi, vegetables, meat, or seafood in a flour and egg batter. There are many kinds of jeon, each with their own flavor. Try a few—you might find a favorite!

STRUCTURE REVIEW

1 Trace over the gray text to get familiar with each sentence. As you write, say the sentences out loud to help with pronunciation and fluency.

A 사장님, 김치전이 어떤 거예요?

B 이거예요. 맛있어요.

A 매워요? 저는 매운 음식을 못 먹어요.

B 하하, 괜찮아요. 이건 많이 안 매워요.

A 아, 그리고 제가 땅콩 알레르기가 있는데요.

B 아이고, 그래요? 땅콩은 안 들어갔어요. 걱정하지 마세요.

A 다행이네요! 그럼 하나 포장해 주세요.

B 네. 잠깐만 기다리세요.

2 Complete the dialogue using the hint words with the appropriate patterns and particles.

A 사장님, ________________?
(김치전, 어떤 거)

B 이거예요. 맛있어요.

A 매워요? ________________.
(저, 매운 음식, 못 먹다)

B 하하, 괜찮아요. 이건 ________________.
(많이, X 맵다)

A 아, 그리고 ________________.
(저, 땅콩 알레르기, 있다)

B 아이고, 그래요? 땅콩은 안 들어갔어요. ________________.
(걱정하다)

A 다행이네요! 그럼 ________________.
(하나, 포장하다)

B 네. 잠깐만 기다리세요.

UNIT 9

Using Public Transportation

대중교통 이용하기

Buses, subways, and taxis are all part of Korea's **대중교통** (public transportation). Apps help, but speaking Korean makes everything smoother and more fun. Let's learn how to ride with confidence!

Key Patterns

- **V-아/어 주세요** PART II - UNIT 12
- **A/V-지요?** PART II - UNIT 15
- **V-(으)세요** PART II - UNIT 18
- **V-(으)ㄹ 수 있어요** PART II - UNIT 22
- **V-(으)ㄹ 거예요** PART II - UNIT 21
- **A-(으)ㄴ데요, V-는데요** PART II - UNIT 25

SCENARIO 1

You're at a bus stop and want to go to Seoul Station. Ask if the bus that's arriving goes there.

CONVERSATION

MP3 92

A 저기 죄송한데요, 이 버스 서울역 가죠?
Excuse me, this bus goes to Seoul Station, right?

B 아니요, 안 가요. 여기는 반대 방향이에요.
No, it doesn't. It's the opposite direction from here.

A 아, 그래요?
Oh, is that so?

B 네, 저쪽 정류장으로 가세요. 저기에서 501번 버스 타세요.
Yes, go to the stop over there. Take bus number 501 at that stop.

A 501번이요? 네, 감사합니다!
Number 501? I see, thank you!

B 아니에요, 조심히 가세요!
You're welcome. Take care!

Practice Tracker

☐ ☐ ☐

Words & Phrases

서울역 [서울력] Seoul Station

반대 방향 opposite direction

정류장 [정뉴장] bus stop

501번 버스 [오배길번 버스] bus number 501

타세요
└ 타다 to get on (vehicles)

조심히 가세요! Take care!

Tip!

In Korea, bus numbers can have 1 to 4 digits, depending on the type of bus. When saying the bus number, add **번** after saying Sino-Korean numbers, like **501번 버스**. You can read the number as a whole (오백일) or digit by digit (오, 공, 일). If it's clear you're talking about buses, people often say just the number with **번**, without saying **버스**.

STRUCTURE REVIEW

1 Trace over the gray text to get familiar with each sentence. As you write, say the sentences out loud to help with pronunciation and fluency.

A 저기 죄송한데요, 이 버스 서울역 가죠?

B 아니요, 안 가요.
여기는 반대 방향이에요.

A 아, 그래요?

B 네, 저쪽 정류장으로 가세요.
저기에서 501번 버스 타세요.

A 501번이요? 네, 감사합니다!

B 아니에요, 조심히 가세요!

2 Complete the dialogue using the hint words with the appropriate patterns and particles.

A 저기 죄송한데요, ____________________?
(이 버스, 서울역, 가다)

B 아니요, ____________________.
(X 가다)

____________________.
(여기, 반대 방향)

A 아, 그래요?

B 네, ____________________.
(저쪽 정류장, 가다)

____________________.
(저기, 501번 버스, 타다)

A 501번이요? 네, 감사합니다!

B 아니에요, ____________________!
(조심히 가다)

SCENARIO 2

You got off at the right subway station, but you're not sure which exit to take. Ask the station staff for help, and also find out how to recharge your transportation card.

CONVERSATION

MP3 93

A 저, '더현대 백화점'에 가고 싶은데요...
Excuse me, I'd like to go to "The Hyundai" Department Store...

B 더현대 백화점이요? 3번 출구로 나가세요.
"The Hyundai" Department Store? Take Exit 3.

저쪽에 숫자 3 보이지요?
That way. See the number 3 over there?

A 아, 보여요. 감사합니다!
Oh, I see it. Thank you!

그리고 카드 충전도 하고 싶은데요.
And I want to recharge my card too.

B 네, 충전은 저쪽에서 기계로 할 수 있어요.
Sure, you can recharge it with the machine over there.

제가 도와드릴게요. 따라 오세요.
I'll help you. Please come with me.

A 감사합니다!
Thank you!

Practice Tracker

☐ ☐ ☐

Words & Phrases

백화점 [배콰점] department store

3번 출구 [삼번 출구] exit 3

숫자 number

충전 charge

기계 machine

도와드릴게요 [도와드릴께요]
└, 도와드리다 to help (honorific)

따라 오세요
└, 따라 오다 to come along

Tip!

In Korean subway stations, exits are marked with numbers, usually inside a yellow square. When talking about exits, we say the number using **Sino-Korean numbers** and add **번 출구**, like **3번 출구** (Exit 3). Subway lines also use Sino-Korean numbers with the word **호선**, such as **2호선** (Line 2) or **4호선** (Line 4).

STRUCTURE REVIEW

1 Trace over the gray text to get familiar with each sentence. As you write, say the sentences out loud to help with pronunciation and fluency.

A 저, 더현대 백화점에 가고 싶은데요...

B 더현대 백화점이요? 3번 출구로 나가세요.
저쪽에 숫자 3 보이지요?

A 아, 보여요. 감사합니다!
그리고 카드 충전도 하고 싶은데요.

B 네, 충전은 저쪽에서 기계로 할 수 있어요.
제가 도와드릴게요. 따라 오세요.

A 감사합니다!

2 Complete the dialogue using the hint words with the appropriate patterns and particles.

A 저, ______________________...
(더현대 백화점, 가고 싶다)

B 더현대 백화점이요? ______________________.
(3번 출구, 나가다)
저쪽에 숫자 3 보이지요?

A 아, ______________________. 감사합니다!
(보이다)
그리고 ______________________.
(카드 충전, 하고 싶다)

B 네, 충전은 저쪽에서 기계로 할 수 있어요.
______________________. ______________________.
(저, 도와드리다) (따라 오다)

A 감사합니다!

SCENARIO 3

You're taking a taxi to Gyeongbokgung Palace. Tell the driver where you're going and ask a simple question about how long the ride will take.

CONVERSATION

MP3 94

A 안녕하세요, 기사님! 경복궁으로 가 주세요.
Hello. Please take me to Gyeongbokgung Palace.

B 네, 알겠습니다.
Alright.

A 여기에서 얼마나 걸릴까요?
How long does it take from here?

B 길이 별로 안 막혀서 20분쯤 걸릴 거예요.
The traffic isn't too bad, so it should take about 20 minutes.

(20 minutes later, you see your destination. Ask the driver to stop here.)

A 아, 여기에서 세워 주세요.
Please stop here.

B 네, 만 원입니다.
That'll be 10,000 won.

A 여기 있어요. 감사합니다. 안녕히 가세요!
Here you go. Thank you. Goodbye!

B 네, 감사합니다. 안녕히 가세요!
Thank you. Goodbye!

Practice Tracker

☐ ☐ ☐

Words & Phrases

경복궁 Gyeongbokgung Palace

알겠습니다 Alright. (formal)

여기에서 얼마나 걸릴까요?
↳ 여기에서 at/from here
↳ 얼마나 how much
↳ 걸리다 to take (time)

길이 별로 안 막혀서 [마켜서]
↳ 길이 막히다 [마키다]
traffic to be heavy

20분쯤 [이십뿐쯤]
↳ 쯤 about

세워 주세요
↳ 세우다 to stop (vehicles)

Tip!

The most common way to give your destination is **[place]로/으로 가 주세요** (Please go to [place]). When you speak to a taxi driver, it's polite to call them **기사님** (driver). In Korean, people often use job titles as polite forms of address.

STRUCTURE REVIEW

1 Trace over the gray text to get familiar with each sentence. As you write, say the sentences out loud to help with pronunciation and fluency.

A 안녕하세요, 기사님! 경복궁으로 가 주세요.

B 네, 알겠습니다.

A 여기에서 얼마나 걸릴까요?

B 길이 별로 안 막혀서 20분쯤 걸릴 거예요.

(20 minutes later, you see your destination. Ask the driver to stop here.)

A 아, 여기에서 세워 주세요.

B 네, 만 원입니다.

A 여기 있어요. 감사합니다. 안녕히 가세요!

B 네, 감사합니다. 안녕히 가세요!

2 Complete the dialogue using the hint words with the appropriate patterns and particles.

A 안녕하세요, 기사님! ________________.
(경복궁, 가다)

B 네, 알겠습니다.

A 여기에서 ________________?
(얼마나, 걸리다)

B 길이 별로 안 막혀서 ________________.
(20분쯤, 걸리다)

(20 minutes later, you see your destination. Ask the driver to stop here.)

A 아, ________________.
(여기, 세우다)

B 네, 만 원입니다.

A 여기 있어요. 감사합니다. 안녕히 가세요!

B 네, 감사합니다. 안녕히 가세요!

UNIT 10

At a Hospital or Pharmacy

병원과 약국 이용하기

It's always a good idea to be prepared. If you're sick or need medicine, knowing some Korean helps a lot. Let's learn how to explain your symptoms at the **병원** (hospital) or **약국** (pharmacy).

Key Patterns

- **V-아/어 주세요** PART II - UNIT 12
- **A/V-았/었어요** PART II - UNIT 14
- **V-(으)세요** PART II - UNIT 18
- **V-지 마세요** PART II - UNIT 19
- **A/V-(으)ㄹ 거예요** PART II - UNIT 21
- **A-(으)ㄴ데요, V-는데요** PART II - UNIT 25

SCENARIO 1

You're feeling sick so you go to a hospital near your home. Talk to the receptionist to check in and explain your symptoms.

CONVERSATION

MP3 95

A 안녕하세요. 예약하셨어요?
Hello. Did you make an appointment?

B 아니요, 안 했어요.
No, I didn't.

A 그러면 여기에 이름, 생년월일, 전화번호 적어 주세요.
그리고 신분증도 보여 주세요.
Then please write your name, date of birth, and phone number here.
And please show me your ID card.

B 네. 여기 있어요.
Okay. Here you go.

A 어디가 안 좋으세요?
What seems to be the problem?

B 머리가 아파요. 그리고 콧물도 나요.
I have a headache, and I have a runny nose.

A 네, 저쪽에서 잠시만 기다리세요.
Okay, please wait over there.

B 감사합니다.
Thank you.

Practice Tracker

☐ ☐ ☐

Words & Phrases

예약하셨어요?
└ 예약하다 to make a reservation

생년월일 date of birth (=생일)

전화번호 phone number

적어 주세요
└ 적다 to write

신분증 [신분쯩] ID card

어디가 안 좋으세요?
What seems to be the problem?
└ 안 좋다 to feel unwell

머리가 아파요
└ 머리가 아프다 to have a headache

콧물도 나요
└ 콧물 [콘물] nasal discharge
└ 콧물이 나다 to have a runny nose

Tip!

Both large and small medical facilities are simply called **병원**. Many clinics and small hospitals allow walk-in visits without a reservation. So if you feel really sick, don't hesitate to go. You can usually get checked right away.

STRUCTURE REVIEW

1 Trace over the gray text to get familiar with each sentence. As you write, say the sentences out loud to help with pronunciation and fluency.

A 안녕하세요. 예약하셨어요?

B 아니요, 안 했어요.

A 그러면 여기에 이름, 생년월일, 전화번호 적어 주세요.
그리고 신분증도 보여 주세요.

B 네. 여기 있어요.

A 어디가 안 좋으세요?

B 머리가 아파요. 그리고 콧물도 나요.

A 네, 알렉스 님. 저쪽에서 잠시만 기다리세요.

B 감사합니다.

2 Complete the dialogue using the hint words with the appropriate patterns and particles.

A 안녕하세요. ____________________? (예약하시다)

B 아니요, ____________________. (X 하다)

A 그러면 여기에 이름, 생년월일, 전화번호 ____________________. (적다)
그리고 신분증도 ____________________. (보이다)

B 네. 여기 있어요.

A ____________________? (어디, 안 좋다)

B ____________________ (머리, 아프다). 그리고 ____________________ (콧물, 나다).

A 네, 알렉스 님. 저쪽에서 잠시만 기다리세요.

B 감사합니다.

SCENARIO 2

You enter the doctor's office after checking in. Explain your symptoms and answer the doctor's simple questions.

CONVERSATION

MP3 96

A 안녕하세요, 알렉스 씨. 어디가 불편하세요?
Hello, Mr. Alex. What's bothering you?

B 머리가 아프고 콧물이 나요. 아, 기침도 해요.
I have a headache and a runny nose. Oh, and I'm coughing too.

A 언제부터 아팠어요?
Since when have you been sick?

B 그저께부터 아팠어요.
Since the day before yesterday.

A 그렇군요. 아이고, 열이 좀 있네요. 약 드릴게요.
I see. Oh, you have a slight fever. I'll prescribe you some medicine.
물 많이 드세요. 그리고 푹 쉬세요.
Drink plenty of water. And get lots of rest.

B 감사합니다.
Thank you.

A 밖에서 잠깐만 기다리세요. 처방전 드릴 거예요.
Please wait outside for a moment. We'll give you the prescription there.

B 네, 감사합니다. 안녕히 계세요.
Okay, thank you. Goodbye.

Practice Tracker

☐ ☐ ☐

Words & Phrases

어디가 불편하세요?
└ 불편하다 to feel unwell

기침도 해요
└ 기침(을) 하다 to cough

열이 좀 있네요
└ 열이 있다 to have a fever

약 medicine

밖 outside

처방전 prescription

Tip!

Just like in many countries, doctors in Korea usually don't give you medicine directly. Instead, they give you a **처방전** (prescription), which you take to a **약국** (pharmacy) to get your medicine. This system applies to both big hospitals and small local clinics. After your consultation, the receptionist will usually print out the prescription for you. You just take it to a nearby pharmacy, and they will prepare your medicine.

STRUCTURE REVIEW

1 Trace over the gray text to get familiar with each sentence. As you write, say the sentences out loud to help with pronunciation and fluency.

A 안녕하세요, 알렉스 씨. 어디가 불편하세요?

B 머리가 아프고 콧물이 나요. 아, 기침도 해요.

A 언제부터 아팠어요?

B 그저께부터 아팠어요.

A 그렇군요. 아이고, 열이 좀 있네요. 약 드릴게요.
물 많이 드세요. 그리고 푹 쉬세요.

B 감사합니다.

A 밖에서 잠깐만 기다리세요. 처방전 드릴 거예요.

B 네, 감사합니다. 안녕히 계세요.

2 Complete the dialogue using the hint words with the appropriate patterns and particles.

A 안녕하세요, 알렉스 씨. ______________________?
(어디, 불편하다)

B 머리가 아프고 콧물이 나요. 아, ______________________.
(기침, 하다)

A 언제부터 아팠어요?

B ______________________.
(그저께, 아프다)

A 그렇군요. 아이고, 열이 좀 있네요. ______________________.
(약, 드리다)
______________________. 그리고 ______________________.
(물, 많이 드시다) (푹 쉬다)

B 감사합니다.

A 밖에서 잠깐만 기다리세요. ______________________.
(처방전, 드리다)

B 네, 감사합니다. 안녕히 계세요.

SCENARIO 3

Let's pick up medicine at the pharmacy. You take your prescription to a pharmacy and the pharmacist explains how to take it.

CONVERSATION

MP3 97

A 안녕하세요. 처방전을 받았는데요.
Hello. I received my prescription.

B 네, 확인할게요. 잠시만요.
Okay, let me check. Just a moment.

(The pharmacist prepares the medicine.)

B 알렉스 님?
Mr. Alex?

A 네.
Yes.

B 약 여기 있어요.
Here's your medicine.

아침, 점심, 저녁 세 번 드세요. 식사 후에 드세요.
Take it three times a day—after breakfast, lunch, and dinner.

A 네. 이 약 졸려요?
Okay. Will this medicine make me sleepy?

B 네, 아마 조금 졸릴 거예요. 운전하지 마세요.
Yes, it might make you a little sleepy. Please don't drive.

그리고 물 많이 드세요. 술은 드시지 마세요.
Also, drink plenty of water. And please don't drink alcohol.

A 네, 감사합니다.
Okay. Thank you.

Practice Tracker

☐ ☐ ☐

Words & Phrases

받았는데요
└ 받다 to receive

확인할게요 [화긴할께요]
└ 확인하다 to check, to confirm

식사 후에 드세요
└ N 후에 after N

졸려요?
└ 졸리다 to be sleepy

아마 maybe

조금 a little

운전하지 마세요
└ 운전하다 to drive

술 alcoholic drinks

Tip!

You can buy medicine without a prescription for mild symptoms, like headaches or colds. The pharmacist will prepare your medicine and explain how to take it. You'll often hear advice like **식사 후에 드세요** (Take it after meals). The opposite of **식사 후에** is **식사 전에** (before meals). On medicine labels or packages, you may also see short forms like **식후** (after meals) and **식전** (before meals).

STRUCTURE REVIEW

1 Trace over the gray text to get familiar with each sentence. As you write, say the sentences out loud to help with pronunciation and fluency.

A 안녕하세요. 처방전을 받았는데요.

B 네, 확인할게요. 잠시만요.

(The pharmacist prepares the medicine.)

B 알렉스 님?

A 네.

B 약 여기 있어요.
아침, 점심, 저녁 세 번 드세요. 식사 후에 드세요.

A 네. 이 약 졸려요?

B 네, 아마 조금 졸릴 거예요. 운전하지 마세요.
그리고 물 많이 드세요. 술은 드시지 마세요.

A 네, 감사합니다.

2 Complete the dialogue using the hint words with the appropriate patterns and particles.

A 안녕하세요. ________________.
(처방전, 받았다)

B 네, 확인할게요. 잠시만요.

(The pharmacist prepares the medicine.)

B 알렉스 님?

A 네.

B 약 여기 있어요. 아침, 점심, 저녁 세 번 드세요. ________________.
(식사 후, 드시다)

A 네. ________________?
(이 약, 졸리다)

B 네, 아마 조금 ________________. ________________.
(졸리다) (운전하다)

그리고 ________________. 술은 ________________.
(물, 많이 드시다) (드시다)

A 네, 감사합니다.

APPENDIX

- Answers
- Index

Answers

PART 1

UNIT 2

Basic Vowels

Essential Practices

1. (1) 아 (2) 요 (3) 오
(4) 여 (5) 아이 (6) 이유

2. (1) 오 
(2) 오이 
(3) 여우 
(4) 이 
(5) 우유 
(6) 아이 

UNIT 3

Basic Consonants

Essential Practices

1. (1) 가 (2) 디 (3) 시
(4) 저 (5) 보리 (6) 머리
(7) 사다 (8) 소나기

2. (1) 나 
(2) 비 
(3) 머리 
(4) 두부 
(5) 아기 
(6) 요리사 

3. (1) 러시아 (2) 바나나 (3) 스위스
(4) 라디오 (5) 아이디어 (6) 모나리자

UNIT 4

Aspirated Consonants & Hard Consonants

Essential Practices

1. (1) 키 (2) 씨 (3) 고리
(4) 따다 (5) 펴 (6) 차요

2. (1) 표 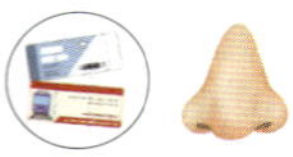
(2) 차 
(3) 싸다 

(4) 오빠 
(5) 비싸다 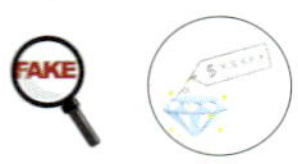

(6) 코끼리 

3. (1) 피자 (2) 토마토 (3) 아파트

UNIT 5

Complex Vowels

Essential Practices

1. (1) 스웨터 (2) 체리 (3) 키위
(4) 샤워 (5) 캐나다 (6) 웨이터

2. (1) 예 (2) 왜 (3) 와
(4) 에 (5) 워 (6) 의

3. (1) 뭐 

(2) 귀 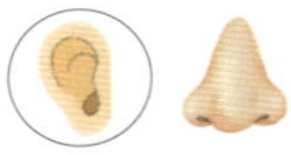
(3) 시계 

(4) 회사 
(5) 추워요 
(6) 돼지 
(7) 사과 
(8) 스웨터 

UNIT 6

Final Consonants "받침"

Essential Practices

1. (1) 숲 (2) 공 (3) 집
(4) 밖 (5) 닻 (6) 낮
(7) 책 (8) 꽃

2. (1) 방 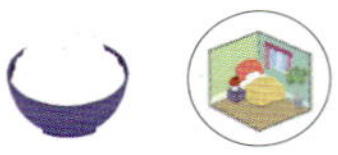
(2) 옷 
(3) 밑 
(4) 공항 
(5) 친구 
(6) 선생님 

3. (1) 치킨 (2) 오렌지 (3) 불고기
(4) 컴퓨터

PART 2

UNIT 2

Basic Markers

Essential Practices

1. (1) 이 - subject (2) 은 - topic
(3) 를 - object (4) 가 - subject
(5) 을 - object (6) 는 - topic

2. (1) 가 (2) 이 (3) 는
(4) 을 (5) 을 (6) 은, 가
(7) 는, 가 (8) 는, 를 (9) 은, 를
(10) 는, 이

3. (1) 가 (2) 는 (3) 를
(4) 은 (5) 을 (6) 이

UNIT 3

Demonstrative Pronouns 이/그/저

Essential Practices

1.

	이 this	그 that	저 that over there
Thing	이것, 이거	그것, 그거	저것, 저거
Person	이 사람, 이분	그 사람, 그분	저 사람, 저분
Place	이곳, 여기	그곳, 거기	저곳, 저기

2. (1) 저걸 (2) 이게 (3) 그건
(4) 저건 (5) 그걸

3. (1) 이 (2) 그 (3) 저
(4) 그 (5) 그

UNIT 4

N이/가 있어요/없어요

Essential Practices

1. (1) 있어요 (2) 없어요
(3) 없어요 (4) 있어요
(5) 있어요

2. (1) 편의점이, 있어요 (2) 파스타가, 없어요
(3) 형이, 없어요, 누나가, 있어요
(4) 오빠가, 없어요, 언니가, 있어요

3. (1) A: 시간 B: 약속, 이, 있어요
(2) A: 화장실, 이, 있어요 B: 저기
(3) A: 오렌지주스(가), 있어요 B: 오렌지주스, 가, 없어요

UNIT 5

N이예요/예요

Essential Practices

1. (1) 예요 (2) 이에요
(3) 이에요 (4) 이에요
(5) 예요

2. (1) 호주 사람이에요 (2) 요리사예요
(3) 회사원이에요 (4) 얼마예요

3. (1) A: 뭐예요 B: 카일이에요
(2) A: 한국 사람이에요 B: 일본 사람이에요
(3) A: 얼마예요 B: 만 원이에요

UNIT 10

A/V-아/어요

Essential Practices

1. 좋다 → 좋아요 맛있다 → 맛있어요
좋아하다 → 좋아해요 가다 → 가요
짜다 → 짜요 보내다 → 보내요
보다 → 봐요 배우다 → 배워요
쓰다* → 써요 바쁘다* → 바빠요
배부르다* → 배불러요 빠르다* → 빨라요

2. (1) 좋아요 (2) 먹어요
(3) 와요 (4) 배불러요
(5) 빨라요 (6) 써요
(7) 바빠요

3. (1) A: 일해요 B: 써요
(2) A: 봐요 B: 바빠요
(3) A: 맛있어요 B: 짜요
(4) A: 배워요 B: 좋아해요
(5) A: 해요 B: 읽어요
(6) A: 마셔요 B: 가요

UNIT 11

안 A/V, 못 V

Essential Practices

1. Negating an Adjective (안)

Basic Form	-아/어요	Negative
좋다	좋아요	안 좋아요
짜다	짜요	안 짜요
바쁘다*	바빠요	안 바빠요
빠르다*	빨라요	안 빨라요
춥다*	추워요	안 추워요
맵다*	매워요	안 매워요

Negating a Verb (안: don't / 못: can't)

Basic Form	-아/어요	don't	can't
먹다	먹어요	안 먹어요	못 먹어요
마시다	마셔요	안 마셔요	못 마셔요
쓰다*	써요	안 써요	못 써요
수영하다	수영해요	수영 안 해요	수영 못 해요
운동하다	운동해요	운동 안 해요	운동 못 해요

Ready-Made Opposites

Basic Form	-아/어요	Negative
알다	알아요	몰라요
있다	있어요	없어요
맛있다	맛있어요	맛없어요
재미있다	재미있어요	재미없어요
영국 사람이다	영국 사람이에요	영국 사람이 아니에요
친구이다	친구예요	친구가 아니에요

2. (1) 안 마셔요 (2) 안 매워요
(3) 안 써요 (4) 요리(를) 안 해요
(5) 못 먹어요

3. (1) 안 추워요 (2) 몰라요
(3) 못 해요 (4) 맛없어요
(5) 아니에요

UNIT 12

V-아/어 주세요

Essential Practices

1. 닫다 → 닫아 주세요
가다 → 가 주세요
기다리다 → 기다려 주세요
확인하다 → 확인해 주세요
쓰다* → 써 주세요
열다 → 열어 주세요
알리다 → 알려 주세요
바꾸다 → 바꿔 주세요
돕다* → 도와주세요

2. (1) 말해 주세요 (2) 도와주세요
(3) 열어 주세요 (4) 닫아 주세요
(5) 가 주세요 (6) 확인해 주세요
(7) 바꿔 주세요 (8) 물, 주세요

3. (1) A: 말해 주세요
(2) A: 봐 주세요
(3) A: 보내 주세요 B: 알려 주세요
(4) B: 김치찌개 A: 기다려 주세요

UNIT 13

V-아/어도 돼요?

Essential Practices

1. 앉다 → 앉아도 돼요
열다 → 열어도 돼요
운동하다 → 운동해도 돼요
들어가다 → 들어가도 돼요
켜다 → 켜도 돼요
시키다 → 시켜도 돼요
입어 보다 → 입어 봐도 돼요
열어 보다 → 열어 봐도 돼요
먹어 보다 → 먹어 봐도 돼요
사진 찍다 → 사진 찍어도 돼요
쓰다* → 써도 돼요
전화하다 → 전화해도 돼요
사다 → 사도 돼요
마시다 → 마셔도 돼요
보다 → 봐도 돼요

2. (1) 써도 돼요 (2) 열어 봐도 돼요
(3) 전화해도 돼요 (4) 포장 돼요
(5) 사진 찍어도 돼요 (6) 입어 봐도 돼요

UNIT 14

A/V-았/었어요

Essential Practices

1. 좋다 → 좋아요 / 좋았어요
재미있다 → 재미있어요 / 재미있었어요
연습하다 → 연습해요 / 연습했어요
피곤하다 → 피곤해요 / 피곤했어요
자다 → 자요 / 잤어요
보내다 → 보내요 / 보냈어요
주다 → 줘요 / 줬어요
배우다 → 배워요 / 배웠어요
부르다* → 불러요 / 불렀어요
빠르다* → 빨라요 / 빨랐어요
아프다* → 아파요 / 아팠어요
쓰다* → 써요 / 썼어요
듣다* → 들어요 / 들었어요
걷다* → 걸어요 / 걸었어요

2. (1) 좋았어요 (2) 보냈어요
(3) 연습했어요 (4) 썼어요
(5) 아팠어요 (6) 걸었어요

3. (1) A: 샀어요 B: 줬어요
(2) A: 했어요 B: 들었어요
(3) A: 재미있었어요 B: 불렀어요
(4) A: 잤어요 B: 피곤했어요
(5) A: 먹었어요 B: 못 먹었어요
(6) A: 감기 걸렸어요 B: 갔어요
A: 먹었어요

UNIT 15
A/V-지요?

Essential Practices

1. (1) 한국 드라마를 좋아하지요
   (2) 케이크가 맛있지요
   (3) 주말 잘 보냈지요
   (4) 감기 걸렸지요
2. (1) 좋지요 (2) 바쁘지요
   (3) 미국 사람이지요 (4) 안 먹지요

UNIT 16
A/V-네요

Essential Practices

1. (1) 여기 커피가 싸네요
   (2) 포도가 다네요
   (3) 인터넷이 빠르네요
   (4) 지수 씨가 일찍 일어났네요
2. (1) 예쁘네요 (2) 덥네요
   (3) 배부르네요 (4) 크네요

UNIT 18
V-(으)세요

Essential Practices

1. 씻다 → 씻으세요 앉다 → 앉으세요
   벗다 → 벗으세요 가다 → 가세요
   보다 → 보세요 기다리다 → 기다리세요
   열다 → 여세요 걸다 → 거세요
   자다 → 주무세요 마시다 → 드세요
   말하다 → 말씀하세요 있다 → 계세요
2. (1) 앉으세요 (2) 씻으세요
   (3) 벗으세요 (4) 조용히 하세요
   (5) 거세요
2. (1) A: 드세요
   (2) B: 주세요 A: 기다리세요
   (3) B: 드세요, 주무세요
   (4) B: 타세요 B: 가세요

UNIT 19
V-지 마세요

Essential Practices

1. (1) 앉지 마세요 (2) 뛰지 마세요
   (3) 타지 마세요 (4) 걸지 마세요
2. (1) 먹지 마세요 (2) 사지 마세요
   (3) 피우지 마세요
   (4) A: 나가지 마세요 B: 걱정하지 마세요

UNIT 20
V-(으)ㄹ까요?

Essential Practices

1. 사진 찍다 → 사진 찍을까요? 먹다 → 먹을까요?
   닫다 → 닫을까요? 쇼핑하다 → 쇼핑할까요?
   가져가다 → 가져갈까요? 만나다 → 만날까요?
   열다 → 열까요? 팔다 → 팔까요?
   만들다 → 만들까요? 굽다* → 구울까요?
   돕다* → 도울까요? 듣다* → 들을까요?
2. (1) 먹을까요 (2) 찍을까요
   (3) 도와드릴까요 (4) 열까요
   (5) 구울까요 (6) 가져갈까요
   (7) 들을까요 (8) 걸을까요

UNIT 21
A/V-(으)ㄹ 거예요

Essential Practices

1.

Basic Form	Present Tense -아/어요	Past Tense -았/었어요	Future Plan, Guess -(으)ㄹ 거예요
하다	해요	했어요	할 거예요
읽다	읽어요	읽었어요	읽을 거예요
만들다	만들어요	만들었어요	만들 거예요
불다	불어요	불었어요	불 거예요
만나다	만나요	만났어요	만날 거예요
듣다*	들어요	들었어요	들을 거예요
걷다*	걸어요	걸었어요	걸을 거예요
굽다*	구워요	구웠어요	구울 거예요
쉽다*	쉬워요	쉬웠어요	쉬울 거예요

2. (1) 갈 거예요 (2) 입을 거예요
   (3) 읽을 거예요 (4) 배울 거예요
   (5) 올 거예요 (6) 불 거예요
   (7) 끝날 거예요
3. (1) B: 안 올 거예요, 불 거예요
   (2) A: 운동할 거예요 B: 쉴 거예요
   (3) A: 살 거예요 B: 구울 거예요
   (4) A: 할 거예요 B: 배울 거예요 B: 재미있을 거예요

UNIT 22
V-(으)ㄹ 수 있어요

Essential Practices

1.

Basic Form	V-(으)ㄹ 수 있어요	V-(으)ㄹ 수 없어요	못 V-아/어요
운전하다	운전할 수 있어요	운전할 수 없어요	운전 못 해요
운동하다	운동할 수 있어요	운동할 수 없어요	운동 못 해요
만나다	만날 수 있어요	만날 수 없어요	못 만나요
읽다	읽을 수 있어요	읽을 수 없어요	못 읽어요
만들다	만들 수 있어요	만들 수 없어요	못 만들어요
걷다*	걸을 수 있어요	걸을 수 없어요	못 걸어요
굽다*	구울 수 있어요	구울 수 없어요	못 구워요

2. (1) A: 입어 볼 수 있어요
(2) A: 불 수 있어요 B: 못 불어요
(3) A: 쓸 수 있어요 B: 쓸 수 있어요
(4) A: 탈 수 있어요 B: 못 타요
(5) A: 만날 수 있어요
(6) A: 먹을 수 있어요 B: 못 먹어요
(7) A: 부를 수 있어요 B: 부를 수 있어요
(8) A: 놀 수 있어요 B: 놀 수 있어요
(9) A: 수영할 수 있어요 B: (수영)할 수 있어요
A: 못 해요

UNIT 23
V-고 싶어요

Essential Practices

1. 걷다 → 걷고 싶어요
닫다 → 닫고 싶어요
사다 → 사고 싶어요
입어 보다 → 입어 보고 싶어요
돕다 → 돕고 싶어요
읽다 → 읽고 싶어요
쇼핑하다 → 쇼핑하고 싶어요
만나다 → 만나고 싶어요
배우다 → 배우고 싶어요

2. (1) 김밥, 먹고 싶어요
(2) 저 영화, 보고 싶지 않아요
(3) 공부하고 싶지 않아요
(4) 운동하고 싶어요
(5) 주스(를/가), 마시고 싶어요
(6) 이 책(을/이), 사고 싶지 않아요
(7) 저 셔츠(를/가), 입어 보고 싶어요
(8) 가족(이), 보고 싶어요
(9) 음악(을/이), 듣고 싶지 않아요

3. (1) 쉬고 싶어요 (2) 배우고 싶어요
(3) 먹고 싶어요 (4) 사고 싶어요
(5) 보고 싶어요 (6) 마시고 싶어요
(7) 여행하고 싶어요

UNIT 24
V-고 있어요

Essential Practices

1. 기다리다 → 기다리고 있어요
가다 → 가고 있어요
자다 → 자고 있어요
일하다 → 일하고 있어요
가르치다 → 가르치고 있어요
요리하다 → 요리하고 있어요
식사하다 → 식사하고 있어요
찾다 → 찾고 있어요
듣다 → 듣고 있어요
배우다 → 배우고 있어요
도와드리다 → 도와드리고 있어요
팔다 → 팔고 있어요

2. (1) 영어(를), 가르치고 있어요
(2) 아침(을), 만들고 계세요
(3) 버스 정류장(을), 찾고 있어요
(4) 한국어(를), 공부하고 있어요
(5) 일기(를), 쓰고 있어요
(6) 신문(을), 읽고 계세요

3. (1) 가고 있어요 (2) 가르치고 있어요
(3) 찾고 있어요 (4) 식사하고 계세요
(5) 듣고 있어요

UNIT 25
A-(으)ㄴ데요, V-는데요

Essential Practices

1. 아프다 → 아픈데요
달다 → 단데요
피곤하다 → 피곤한데요
더럽다* → 더러운데요
굽다 → 굽는데요
재미있다 → 재미있는데요
할 수 있다 → 할 수 있는데요
예약했어요 → 예약했는데요
작다 → 작은데요
필요하다 → 필요한데요
사고 싶다 → 사고 싶은데요
덥다* → 더운데요
맛있다 → 맛있는데요
없다 → 없는데요
시켰어요 → 시켰는데요

2. (1) 방이 더러운데요 (2) 수건이 없는데요
(3) 백화점을 찾고 있는데요 (4) 이거 사고 싶은데요
(5) 배가 아픈데요 (6) 현금이 없는데요

3. (1) 사고 싶은데요 (2) 쓰고 싶은데요
(3) 찾고 있는데요 (4) 예약했는데요
(5) 시켰는데요

Index

ㅇ

ㅌ

ㅍ

ㅎ

ETC.

Memo

My KOREAN TUTOR for Ultimate Beginners

Written by	Saemi Park, Kyuin Kim
Translated by	Jamie Lypka
First Published	November, 2025
First Printing	November, 2025
Publisher	Kyu-do Chung
Editor-in-Chief	Suk-hee Lee
Editor	Hyeon-soo Lee, Jihee Han
Cover Design	Soo jung Koo
Interior Design	Soo jung Koo, Hyun-ju Yoon
Illustrated by	Chang-hoon Ji
Voice Actor	Rae-whan Kim, So-yun Shin, Word Cameron Lee

DARAKWON
Darakwon Bldg., 211 Munbal-ro, Paju-si
Gyeonggi-do, Republic of Korea 10881
Tel : 02-736-2031 Fax : 02-732-2037
(Marketing Dept. ext.: 250~252, Editorial Dept. ext.: 420~426)

ISBN : 978-89-277-3355-3 13710

http://www.darakwon.co.kr
http://koreanbooks.darakwon.co.kr

Visit the Darakwon homepage to learn about our other publications and promotions and to download the contents in MP3 format.